THE END IS MUSIC

CASCADE COMPANIONS

The Christian theological tradition provides an embarrassment of riches: from scripture to modern scholarship, we are blessed with a vast and complex theological inheritance. And yet this feast of traditional riches is too frequently inaccessible to the general reader.

The Cascade Companions series addresses the challenge by publishing books that combine academic rigor with broad appeal and readability. They aim to introduce nonspecialist readers to that vital storehouse of authors, documents, themes, histories, arguments, and movements that comprise this heritage with brief yet compelling volumes.

TITLES IN THIS SERIES:

Reading Augustine by Jason Byassee
Conflict, Community, and Honor by John H. Elliott
An Introduction to the Desert Fathers by Jason Byassee
Reading Paul by Michael J. Gorman
Theology and Culture by D. Stephen Long
Creation and Evolution by Tatha Wiley
Theological Interpretation of Scripture by Stephen Fowl
Reading Bonhoeffer by Geffrey B. Kelly
Justpeace Ethics by Jarem Sawatsky
Feminism and Christianity by Caryn D. Griswold
Angels, Worms, and Bogeys by Michelle A. Clifton-Soderstrom
Christianity and Politics by C. C. Pecknold
A Way to Scholasticism by Peter S. Dillard
Theological Theodicy by Daniel Castelo
The Letter to the Hebrews in Social-Scientific Perspective
     by David A. deSilva
Basil of Caesarea by Andrew Radde-Galwitz
A Guide to St. Symeon the New Theologian by Hannah Hunt
Reading John by Christopher W. Skinner

THE END IS MUSIC

A Companion to Robert W. Jenson's Theology

CHRIS E. W. GREEN

CASCADE *Books* · Eugene, Oregon

THE END IS MUSIC
A Companion to Robert W. Jenson's Theology

Cascade Companions

Cascade Books
An Imprint of Wipf and Stock Publishers
199 W. 8th Ave., Suite 3
Eugene, OR 97401

www.wipfandstock.com

PAPERBACK ISBN: 978-1-4982-9082-1
HARDCOVER ISBN: 978-1-4982-9084-5
EBOOK ISBN: 978-1-4982-9083-8

Cataloging-in-Publication data:

Names: Green, Chris E. W., author.

Title: The end is music : A companion to Robert W. Jenson's theology / Chris E. W. Green.

Description: Eugene, OR: Cascade Books | Cascade Companions | Includes bibliographical references.

Identifiers: ISBN: 978-1-4982-9082-1 (paperback) | ISBN: 978-1-4982-9084-5 (hardcover) | ISBN: 978-1-4982-9083-8 (ebook).

Subjects: LCSH: Jenson, Robert W. | Theology.

Classification: BX8080 J44 G74 2018 (print) | BX8080 (ebook).

Manufactured in the U.S.A.   MARCH 5, 2018

Contents

Preface

It is exceedingly difficult to write an adequate introduction or companion to a theologian's work. This is perhaps especially true in cases where the theologian has written as much as Robert Jenson has written, and when their thought is as demanding and unusual as his certainly, and perhaps notoriously, is. Some would argue that writing about another's work is also inevitably complicated—if not compromised from the beginning—by either intense dislike for or intense devotion to it. All to say, it is virtually impossible to represent someone's work fairly. So why try such a thing?

In the first place, there is no better way to honor a theologian's contribution than by offering a critical and appreciative interpretation of it. I certainly mean to do just that: I owe a debt to Robert Jenson and his theology, and this book is one way of acknowledging that debt. Writing an introduction or companion to another's work also provides readers who happen to be interested in Jenson the opportunity to gain new perspective on or insight into his work. Anyway, I know that I have learned from others' readings of Jenson—including those readings I find incredible and appalling, as well as those I find persuasive and enchanting.

On that note, I have to say that I find much of the criticism of Jenson's work not only unfortunate but even unwarranted. It is something like criticizing the Brooklyn Bridge for not being in London or Saint Paul's Cathedral for not being built over water. Of course, it goes without saying that I do find serious problems with some of Jenson's theological claims and maneuvers. But in this book I am trying to describe his work as charitably and faithfully as I can so that it appears in its own best light and as a gift to the church. It may very well be, as Jenson has said, that every theologian's system is destined to be dismembered piece by piece and used up in ongoing debates. However, this is my attempt to envision the system as a whole and to recommend it as a beautiful, glorious word about the God we adore and the gospel we have been entrusted with. I have, as I said, a debt to him. If I can draw some others into the same indebtedness, then I will be doubly pleased.

Writing about a theology is inseparably bound up with what happens to you when you are reading it. What did the reading do to you? How did it wound? How did it heal? How did it bother? How did it enthuse? How did it confound? How did it illuminate? These are the things that move one to write. What is more, writing a book like this one is perhaps the best way to learn truly how a theology works, how it hangs together as a whole. Readers of Jenson already know that he himself did it with Karl Barth and Jonathan Edwards; so, on this score I am merely imitating him.

I would not have been able to begin this project, much less complete it, without the constant encouragement of my wife, Julie, and feedback from friends—in particular, Steve Wright and Fr. Al Kimel. While on sabbatical, I met weekly with a group of students, colleagues, and friends for an informal seminar on Jenson's theology. I am deeply indebted to them as well, for their remarks on and proofreading of early drafts of these chapters. In no particular order, then, thanks to Zach Bennett, Justin Arnwine, Fr. Kenneth Tanner, Silas and Abby Sham, Christopher Wayne Brewer, and Danielle Larson. This work is dedicated to you.

INTRODUCTION

HOW (NOT) TO READ THEOLOGY

There are any numbers of ways to read a theologian's work, some acceptable and others unacceptable; some disciplined, and others lazy; some beneficial and others harmful. At the risk of creating yet another typology,[1] I might suggest for heuristic purposes the following forms as characteristic of undisciplined reading: (a) *hagiographical* readings seek out passages that cast a theologian, her work, or both in the best possible light; at the exact opposite extreme, (b) *combative* readings seek out passages that (at least seem to) indicate the inadequacy or malignancy of a theological text or system; (c) *exploitative* readings, the favored strategy of gifted students and deadline-facing scholars, make raids on theological sources in search of "proof texts" that validate or invalidate some aspect of an argument; (d) *exploratory* readings are less violent, less consumerist, less rushed than these other undisciplined types, wandering more or less aimlessly through various sources with an eye out for anything especially beautiful or particularly useful. Disciplined theological reading, by contrast, takes one or more of the following forms: (e) *diagnostic,* (f) *evaluative,* or (g) *formative*: the first approach works painstakingly to identify the

---

1. For good reason, my friend Tony Hunt laments, "Of the creation of typologies there is no end."

key features of a theologian's thought as well as the origins of those ideas and the trajectories of their developments over time; the second approach passes judgment on the worthiness or unworthiness of parts or the whole of a theologian's contribution; and the last posture seeks to engage a theologian's thought in ways that train the imagination for skillful and faithful theological work.

My own reading of Jenson began as exploration, spurred on by Stanley Hauerwas's suggestion that Jenson has been one of the most important contemporary theologians. But it quickly turned to something more serious. For years, I read and taught Jenson with theological and spiritual formation in mind—my own, as well as my students'. Eventually, however, thanks to questions from my students that I could not satisfactorily answer, and periodic conversational back-and-forth with friends and colleagues who also were reading Jenson,[2] I realized I had to make my way through all of his works again, asking not only what they evoked in and made possible for me, but also how they held together as a whole, and whether or not his system worked on its own terms as an articulation of Christian reality. What I have written here is the upshot of all that reading and the many conversations that it generated along the way.

THE WAYS OF JENSON'S THEOLOGY

Jenson's work is easy to misread, and it often has been misunderstood and misrepresented, even by capable and sympathetic scholars. This should not be too surprising, given how much he published over his career; the peculiarity of his reasoning; his creative interpretations of biblical,

---

2. Especially Stephen Wright, without whose encouragement and direction this book would almost certainly never have been written.

theological, and philosophical texts;[3] his reluctance to explain what he does not mean; and the density of his writing style. But many misreadings of Jenson result from the failure to appreciate how his thinking works. Unless readers are willing to engage patiently and carefully enough to get some sense of the overall shape and movement of Jenson's project, the encompassing architecture and its internal dynamics, it will prove exceedingly difficult, if not in fact impossible, to understand any aspect of it.

His project, in one sense, is astonishingly ambitious. As Jenson frequently acknowledged, he attempted nothing less than a revision of the entire sweep of Christian dogmatics, beginning with a dramatic reimagining of what it means for God to be the Trinity revealed in the story the church tells about Jesus. Right from the beginning of his career, he at every turn called into question and offered alternatives to received notions of what it means for God to be who and what the gospel of Jesus's kingdom claims that he is. But, on closer examination, at the heart of Jenson's work are a handful of metaphysical and methodological insights that by and large determine the structure and direction of his entire project. In another sense, then, Jenson's work is remarkably modest. We might say he wants simply to witness what happens to Christian dogma and praxis when these few insights about God and creation are given their full sway.[4] Or, as Stephen Wright puts it, using Isaiah Berlin's famous analogy, Jenson is a hedgehog and not a fox: he knows and cares about only one thing.

3. As Pannenberg and others have noted, Jenson is an immensely learned theologian. But it is impossible at times to tell the difference between his innovation and his traditionalism due to the ways he reads other theologians' works (from Gregory of Nyssa to Jonathan Edwards).

4. In an early essay, he claims he is "more and more occupied with identifying the simplest, most rudimentary utterances of the faith."

Eugene Rogers has described Jenson's method as "mathematical," a description that strikes very close to the truth. Jenson often does apply his central commitments like a theorem to whatever theological and ethical concerns grasp his attention. Perhaps a musical analogy works even better than the mathematical one. Take, for example, Arvo Pärt's tintinnabuli method, a compositional technique that involves various inversions of a particular chord. Pärt's music begins with a fundamental note, takes up the triad associated with it, and then moves on to the harmonics made possible by that triad. Throughout the piece, that triad remains the "tonal center," as what Pärt calls the "melody voice" and "triad voice" complete each other. As Orthodox theologian Peter Bouteneff puts it, once Pärt establishes rules and structures for a given piece, the music (so to speak) composes itself. Jenson's theology, I'm convinced, works much the same way. Beginning with a set of insights, Jenson works through whatever issue or theme takes his attention (e.g., creation or salvation, pneumatology or eschatology) by asking how these commitments change the usual understanding so that the gospel can be spoken more faithfully here and now.

At the risk of oversimplification and conceptual elision, we can perhaps figure the determinative moves of Jenson's "compositional technique" in the following statements: (a) he holds to an understanding of God's being as, like a meaningful conversation or a good story, an inherently lively and dramatic event; in his own words, "God is what happens between Jesus and his Father in their Spirit";[5] (b) he insists that creaturely reality is "bespoken reality," determined to be meaningful and good just by the dramatic coherence of the divine conversation about us and dialog with us, an insistence that requires (c) a revisionary

5. Jenson, *Systematic Theology*, 1:75.

metaphysical account of God's being in relation to creation as not time*less* but time*ly*; in this scheme, God is not sheer duration, but lively presence, and creation exists just as the time God takes for us; (d) he contends, in affirmation of the traditional Creator/creature distinction, that our history with God is also God's history with us, and (e) he upholds with the strictest Cyrillean christological logic that God has decided to be freely and fully available to and identified with creation in that history in the person of the Israelite Jesus, who is head of the *totus Christus*, an identification so absolute and comprehensive that (f) whatever happens to Jesus thereby happens to all creatures as they are drawn by the Spirit into his own relation to the Father—even now by anticipation of what is promised in the end.

Identifying God

Jenson is concerned above all with *identifying* God, a concern born from struggles to keep his faith through his undergraduate studies.[6] From the very beginning of his career, therefore, he insisted that the gospel is good news only if we know *who* is presented to us in the gospel-proclamation. As he often put it, the news that, say, Stalin is raised from the dead would not be good for many, and certainly not for everyone and everything. That question, of course, forces another, which the young Jenson also recognized: *how* is this one true God identifiable? Where do we find him? How do we distinguish him from all the other possible gods? For identification to take place, Jenson concluded, God must make himself *concretely available*; that is, as he would say later, "he must be present to [us] in [our] space."[7] And to do that, God must be *embodied* for us so that we are able to

6. Jenson, "Theological Autobiography," 47.
7. Jenson, *Systematic Theology*, 2:48.

point to him and say, "*There* is God." For God to be so available, therefore, everything depended on the presence to us of the risen Christ "concrete in time and space, centrally on the Eucharistic table."[8] In coming to these commitments, Jenson was "Lutheran" even before he read Luther, and he continued to hold to them throughout his career.

Time and the Event of Being Present

Jenson's doctoral work at Heidelberg (under the direction of Peter Brunner) focused on the doctrine of election in Barth's *Church Dogmatics*. Jenson was the first to recognize that the notion of eternity's relation to time in *CD* II/1 is the "ruling center" of Barth's work, and that the doctrine radically "upend[s] traditional understandings of the relation between time and eternity and thus inaugurate[s] an innovative ontology."[9] Jenson's development of Barth's doctrine was from the beginning the ruling center of his own project as well, and energized his attempts at carrying out the innovative ontology Barth inaugurated.

During this same time, Jenson adopted Brunner's "bit of speculation" that God's history with creatures is God's *own* history, which when paired with Barth's radical notion of God's relation to time yielded for Jenson an understanding of God's life as a *dramatic event*—a happening with a beginning, a dramatic development full of "detours" and other surprises, and a fulfilling end. Jenson was convinced that however strange such a claim may seem at first, and whatever reworking of received metaphysics and theological assumptions it requires, it is nonetheless necessary to maintain. Most of his work, therefore, has been concerned

8. Jenson, "Theological Autobiography," 47.

9. Jenson, "D. Stephen Long's *Saving Karl Barth*," 132.

with showing why it is necessary, and how such a vision of God's life might be articulated intelligibly and faithfully.

Sheer availability does not make identification possible, however. Learning for human beings is always temporal, so God must live with us over time in such a way that we may learn what he is like. Only after we have lived with God long enough and closely enough to be able testify to his character can we answer faithfully the questions put to us about his identity. In the history of Israel, and especially in the life and death of a certain trouble-making Galilean peasant, God does in fact live with us in ways that can be known, as he makes himself available to be seen and to be heard, present to act and to be acted on.

All history happens within the unfolding of the will of God, to be sure, but by God's will only certain events within that history reveal God to us. God is identified not only in these certain events but also with them. Ultimately, Jesus's life (a life that includes Israel's and the church's) is the particular history that speaks of God, and it does so precisely because the events of Jesus's life are simply the events of God being God in reach of us. Therefore, whatever we learn of God, we necessarily learn it from Jesus and what happens with him.

Telling the Story Promisingly

Because God's life is itself dramatic, his history with us makes a *story*, one with a recognizable (if at times bizarrely twisted) plot.[10] It is that story that is given to us when Israel's Scriptures are read in ways fitted to the New Testament's witness to Jesus. And it is knowing that story that in turn enables our witness to God. When we are asked how

10. Jenson thanks his wife, Blanche, for keeping this commitment always on his mind.

to identify the true God, the story gives us an answer: God is whoever delivered Israel from Egypt and raised Jesus from the dead. When we are asked how we know that this God is good and wise and just, the story gives us an answer: because in Christ's sufferings he triumphs over injustice, evil, and death, and because in Christ's victory he opens the future to us with the unconditional promise of a share in his own abundant life.

A creature, Jenson insists, following Luther, is nothing other than a created word of God that answers to the uncreated Word whose image we are made to share. We exist at all because we are spoken to and about by God. We can trust this existence ultimately to be good because we are spoken to and about by the Trinity revealed in the life of Jesus. But given that we do so exist, and that the God whom Jesus reveals is both our loving origin and our beatific destiny, we can talk lovingly and beautifully to and about God and to and about one another.

But we must learn to speak and to listen as God does. Now, in this time between the times, all human speech comes finally either to law or to gospel. The one binds by command and demand; the other frees by unconditional promise. The one determines the present by a closed past; the other determines the present by an open future. For Jenson, the gospel works as gospel only as we (again and again, in new situations and contexts) learn to speak about what God has done in ways that move people toward the glad future they've been promised. Any so-called proclamation of the gospel that does not actually effect freedom for others is in fact only "law."

We can truly speak as God speaks, because through the resurrection of Jesus all things are possible for us. As Jenson puts it time and again, what *will* happen (in the end), *can* happen (in the here and now). Believers can afford the risks of love because the one who is at work among us is present to us from the far side of death, and because we are sure that when all is said and done, he will take us to himself. Where he is, we will be also.

The Sense of an Ending

In the end, we, with all creation, will be taken into God. This means we will be judged—not so much rewarded or punished as *rectified*. "Judgment," Jenson insists, "is the act that restores the community to its right order."[11] And when God is the judge and all creation is the judged, everyone and everything is once for all put to rights. Now, we pray as we were taught to pray, "Father, let your will be done on earth as it is in heaven." So long as history lasts, God's people will continue to pray that prayer. When God finally answers that prayer, history ends (not in termination, but in fulfillment, in translation into God's own life). Then, God will be through doing all that God has to do for creation to be all that God intended it to be. Then, the joys begin. "The end is music"[12]—and dancing.

If these are in fact the conceptual moves that Jenson's "compositional technique" relies upon, how does he characteristically put them to use? How does his method actually work? A couple of examples should make the point, and prepare the way for closer study of Jenson's theology. First, in his proposed vision of Christ and Trinity for the Muslim world, Jenson begins with the notion of the prophet in Islamic theology and asks what it would mean if such a prophet, in a departure from received Islamic tradition, were truly risen from the dead and if the spirit of that prophet were in fact God's own Spirit, so that the prophet

11. Jenson, *Systematic Theology*, 2:324.

12. Ibid., 2:369.

spoke from a wholly new creaturely reality both for God to creatures and to God as a creature.[13] He concludes that what follows from those two suppositions would be everything required for a faithful Trinitarian and christological confession in Islamic contexts. Second, and similarly, in his reflections on the legitimacy and necessity of prayer to Mary, the Mother of God, Jenson contends that God, in order to be known and loved, must have a space among us, a place where he is available to be seen and heard and touched. Heaven is such a place, he believes, as was Israel's temple, and, later, Israel's prophets and, later still, Israel's scriptures. Last in that line, Mary too is a "created space for God."[14] As *mater dei*, the "Container of the Uncontainable," she is in her own person heaven and temple and prophet and scripture. Therefore, Jenson concludes, "After all the Lord's struggle with his beloved Israel, he finally found a place in Israel that unbelief would not destroy like the Temple, or silence like the prophets, or simply lose, like the Book of the Law before Josiah. This place is a person. To ask Mary to pray for us is to meet him there."[15]

In these examples, the outlines of Jenson's usual theological moves are perhaps unusually clear. His arguments are not always this tightly drawn, but they do always follow a comparable logic. And once this method, or compositional technique, is understood, Jenson's work as a whole and in its parts begins to make a more comprehensible sense.

THE COHERENCE OF JENSON'S PROJECT

Jenson had a long and productive career. As a result, those who are interested in his work have to decide how all that

13. Jenson, "Risen Prophet," 57–67.
14. Jenson, "Space for God," 56.
15. Ibid.

he has written fits together. Is there an early Jenson to be distinguished from a mature Jenson? If so, how does the early work fit with the later work? What changes or developments demark the early and the mature? Does he, as some have suggested, shift away from his radical political and theological beginnings? Does he become over time increasingly conservative and "Catholic"? Does he switch sides in the culture wars?

As I read him, there *is* a difference to be made between Jenson's early and later work. *Story and Promise* (1973), in my judgment, should be regarded as the first work of the mature Jenson. But the discontinuities from his earlier work are relatively slight and all too easily exaggerated. Politically, he does not repudiate or abandon the radicalism of his youth in relation to issues such as race, militarism, and the American dream, although he does shift his focus to what he deems pressing social and cultural concerns—such as abortion, euthanasia, and same-sex marriage—that bring him into alignment with conservatives on these particular issues.[16] Theologically, he refines his articulations over time and takes up engagement with new conversation partners, but he never abandons the core commitments that shaped his earliest works.[17] So, at least as I see it, it is best to read

16. Jenson differs from these conservatives most, perhaps, in his refusal of the nationalism that characterizes much of their thought.

17. These developments, or at least the need for them, are often obvious. See, for example, "Eschatological Politics and Political Eschatology," an early article (published in 1969) that includes the admission that he has just begun the work needed to think through his eschatological claims, and "Bride of Christ," a late one (published in 2011 Festschrift for Carl Braaten) that acknowledges a major omission in his *Systematics*. For other examples, see his response in *Dialog* to H. Paul Santmire's critique of *Religion against Itself* (1968), his work on Satan, "Evil as Person" (1989), "Second Thoughts about Theologies of Hope" (2000), "Second Thought about Inspiration" (2004), and his renunciation of what he claims is a major pseudo-question

Jenson's work before *Story and Promise* as groundwork for
what comes in that book and after it. And, again as I see it, it
is best to read his *Systematics* and the other dogmatic works
alongside the scriptural commentary, the philosophical
works, and the cultural criticism. The more widely he is
read, the more deeply he can be understood.

---

in "Ipse Pater Non Est Impassibilis" (2009). See also his own account
given in "Reversals," 30–33.

1

GOD

Identification & Event

Christian speech is concerned, first and foremost, with identifying God. As Jenson puts it, everything we have to say about anything is ultimately an elaboration of who and what we understand God to be. And that means we have no hope of proclaiming the gospel faithfully unless we know how to "intend the specific reality"[1] that is God. The problem is, there is an endless number of gods on offer; and by itself the word "God" is so elastic that it can be stretched to mean almost anything. Besides all that, we are at every turn tempted to make a God in our own image, a God who fits our needs. The first great religious question, then, is not "*Does* God exist?" but "*Which* God is truly God?"[2] Out of all the gods described in the various religious and spiritual discourses, which one truly answers to reality? Which one can actually get done for us what the gospel promises?[3]

1. Jenson, *Systematic Theology,* 1:42.

2. Jenson, *Large Catechism,* 7.

3. As Jenson liked to put it in German, "Was heisst, Gott?"

13

THE EVENTS OF GOD'S IDENTIFICATION

The good news is that the living and true God identifies himself to us. According to Israel's and the church's witness, God presents himself to us in particular historical events, making himself available to be known in certain ways at specific times and specific places. For Jenson, this claim about God's identifiability entails (at least) three critical affirmations: (1) because God makes himself *available*, we can in and through these events begin to know him, distinguishing him from other putative and so-called gods and from the figments of our own imaginings; (2) because *God* makes himself available, the events create an identifiable history, a narrative that truly reveals the character of the one who has acted in these ways; and (3) in this availability, God indeed *makes himself* who and what he is. God, just by being God, both exists and creates and saves what he creates into his own existence. The event of God's life with God and the event that is God's life with creation are truly one event. What God is for himself includes what God is for creation. It could not be otherwise if the gospel of Jesus's incarnation and resurrection is true.

The apostolic witness given in the New Testament lays down the first rule for all truly Christian identifications of God: "God is whoever raised Jesus from the dead, having before raised Israel from Egypt."[4] Again, in Jenson's formulation, all of these terms are crucial and equally important. We cannot talk about this *God* without talking about this Israelite Jesus and his being raised from the dead. But we also cannot talk about *Jesus*, or his people, Israel, without talking about this God who delivers Jesus from the death that had claimed him and all other creatures. And we cannot talk about *resurrection* without talking about the God

4. Jenson, *Systematic Theology*, 1:63.

of *Israel* and the promise he keeps in raising Jesus from the grave as he had raised Jesus's ancestors from Egypt.

Against the force of much contemporary theological pressure, Jenson contends that God is "*intrinsically knowable.*"[5] But the word *God* by itself is so ambiguous that it means more or less nothing. Even if we avoid that problem by identifying God with a proper name—say, YHWH or Father, Son, and Spirit—we still need identifying descriptions. Names, in other words, work to identify only as and through *story*. Or, more precisely, they depend upon the kind of coherence that only dramatics makes possible. Drama, after all, is a narrative carried along by conversation and dialog—and that is exactly the kind of reality that creatures inhabit with God.

"The uniqueness of God is narratively established."[6] And so we have to know the determining events of the divine history with us if we hope to recognize the one the divine name actually identifies. This is why, for Jenson, telling the one story that the Scriptures tell is nothing less than *mandatory* for those who wish to worship the God revealed in Christ. Without that story, Christian claims about God's being, purpose, and character, as well as the biblical accounts of divine action and the invocations and petitions found in the church's spiritual and liturgical traditions, are simply irreconcilably conflicted.[7] If, then, we hope to speak the same gospel the prophets and apostles spoke, if we hope to identify for ourselves and for the others the God the canonical Scriptures specify, then we must let the story of what happened with Israel and with Jesus, as Israel-in-person, determine our claims from first to last.

5. Jenson, *Systematic Theology*, 1:224.

6. Jenson, "The Father, He," 99.

7. Jenson, *Systematic Theology*, 1:64.

THE IDENTIFICATION OF GOD AS EVENT

Jenson holds that the Scriptures tell one story because there is one story to be told. And there is one story to be told because God is one. Or, as Andrew Nichol puts it, "there is one story because there is one God whose very act and being provides the narrative coherence in what appears an otherwise disparate story."[8] In a word, dramatic coherence is possible for our history because God's life is itself dramatically coherent. God's own life has a narrative structure: this is the significance of the Trinitarian relations. Therefore, as God happens to creation, history itself becomes meaningful and storyable.

In Jenson's vision, God is identifiable with and by events in our history because God's own life is event,[9] the (only) kind of uncreated event that creates without in any way violating either its own integrity or the integrity of what it creates. But what does it mean to talk about God in these terms? And how does such talk matter for the church's preaching and prayer? A difference between Jenson and Moltmann on this score proves instructive. As Moltmann articulates it,

> there is in fact no "personal God" projected in heaven. But there are persons in God: the Son, the Father, and the Spirit. In that case one does not simply pray to God as a heavenly Thou, but prays *in* God. One does not pray to an event but *in* this event. One prays through the Son to the Father in the Spirit.[10]

Jenson, by contrast, holds that we pray both in and to God. The "persons" of the Trinity are precisely in the

8. Nichol, *Exodus and Resurrection*, 33.

9. Jenson, *Systematic Theology*, 1:221.

10. Moltmann, *Crucified God*, 365.

structure of their mutual relations one personal God. He holds to this commitment because he believes that the language of the Scriptures demands it, as does the religious and spiritual life mandated by the gospel. "The Bible's language about God is drastically personal":[11] God is said to change his mind, to act and react, to make threats and then to withdraw them, to make promises and then fulfill them in utterly surprising ways. So, if we reject all this language as simply inappropriately anthropomorphic, we cannot rightly identify or know the God of the Scriptures.

But how can an *event* be a *person*? As Jenson sees it, a person, whether divine or human, is quite simply many events as one event, many occasions drawn together as one coherent happening. That is, a person is someone whose story, when finished, makes sense as a whole. We know through the incarnation-event that this is true both of God and of human beings, and we know that only because God is a person in that sense that we can be persons at all. God, by being personal, creates persons who can be personal with each other as well as with him. For us, nothing is more personal than prayers of need. And for God, nothing is more personal than responses to those needs and the prayers they generate. Therefore, as Jenson will say again and again, "unabashed petitionary prayer is the one decisively appropriate creaturely act over against the one true God."[12] Prayer names the way creatures enter into the conversation that God personally is, dialoging with each other and with him.

THE IDENTITIES OF GOD'S ACT

When speaking of God, Jenson as a rule prefers the language of "identities" to "persons." There are, he wants to

11. Jenson, *Systematic Theology*, 1:222.
12. Ibid.

say, three *identities* in the one *act* of God. Hence, to speak meaningfully about the one God, we have to work out all our statements in three interconnected ways. If we hope to say how God is good, for example, we have to say that God is good like a *giver* is good, good like a *gift* is good, and good like the *outcome* of a gift given and received is good. Or, if we hope to talk about God as love, we have to "run the predicate across all three identities" by saying how that love is the beginning ("Father"), presence (Jesus), and fulfilment ("Spirit") of all things. Insofar as we remain faithful to the gospel, we won't speak of God as "love-in-general." We will, instead, insist that God is *Jesus's* love—the love he shares with the Father and with us in the one Spirit—as the source and goal of our lives. The same pattern holds true for all Christian theologizing. Whatever the doctrine of divine simplicity is taken to mean, it cannot mean that the triune identities make no difference for talking about God.[13]

Jenson insists that Christians necessarily specify God by appeal to these three identities precisely because time, which fundamentally conditions human existence, has three identities. In the Scriptures we find that "God is . . . identified by a narrative that uses the tense-structure of ordinary language, rather than by time-neutral characters, as in 'God is whoever is omnipotent.'"[14] As creatures, we are bounded in time by God, who as our Creator, is our past, present, and future. In Pauline language, we come from Christ, are held together in him, and are ultimately reconciled into our destiny with him. Therefore, attempts to identify the gospel's God require us to "point with all three of time's arrows."[15] God not only gives us time—a beginning and an end that open up a present—but also gives our lives

13. Jenson, "Hidden and Triune God," 7.

14. Jenson, "Three Identities in One Action," 2.

15. Ibid., 4.

in that time meaning and purpose. God gives us a good beginning and a good end "rhymed" in a good present.

To identify the gospel's God, we must identify Jesus. And to do that, we have to acknowledge the ways that God's self-revelation is temporally structured. The temptation is to abstract to a timeless God, a God beyond our history, a God unaffected by what happens in time. But such a God could not and would not take on flesh as one of us. Such a God could not and would not suffer and die for us. Such a God could not and would not share an identity with us. If the gospel is true, then God simply cannot be sheerly immune to time, essentially and necessarily removed from our history. God, by his own free decision, must share a history with us, so that what happens to us happens to him, and vice versa. "The reality of Christ, his death, resurrection, and present Lordship, is not merely a set of events within what is created by some other act of God. It is a Trinitarian identity of the one act of God by which the world is."[16]

Jesus

This is perhaps best expressed in a characteristic Jensonian axiom: God is what happens with Jesus. What are we to make of this claim? Basically this: Jesus, living in our time as one of us, experienced God as his "past" and his "future," that is, as the transcendent givenness and the transcendent goal that afforded his life its definition. And because Jesus himself is God-as-a-creature, his experience determines the reality of all other creatures. Jesus, God-in-the-flesh, both trusts in God as the ground of his being and hopes in God as the realization of his fullness, and just so lives lovingly with God in the present. By living in that way, he draws us into his own share in the divine life. Said another way, the

16. Jenson, "Creation as Triune Act," 41.

enfleshed Word is not only God but also another than God, and therefore enjoys a unique relation to the Father and to the Spirit—the very relation we are created to share. It is precisely because of the eternal difference in the divine life between Father, Son, and Spirit that Jesus can remain one with the Father even in "the most radical state of 'otherness' from God or separation from God." Without this divine identity-in-difference, God's life could not "open" to that which is not-God. Creation—and, of course, salvation—would be strictly impossible.

Jenson holds, in his own words, to a "hyper-Cyrillean" Christology.[17] He wants, at every point, to keep the focus on *Jesus*, the enfleshed Son. He maintains it as axiomatic: Christology begins not with an account of the two natures and their interaction but with the life-events of "the one protagonist of the gospels."[18] Above all, we must avoid separating the Word from Jesus. The Word does not "become flesh" in the sense that he becomes someone he was not. The gospel requires us to insist that Jesus and the Word are one and the same person, however difficult it may be to explain how that can be so.

> In whatever way the Son may antecede his conception by Mary, we must not posit the Son's antecedent subsistence in such fashion as to make the incarnation the addition of the human Jesus to a Son who was himself without him. By the dogma, Mary is the mother of God the Son, she is Theotokos, and not of a man who is united with God the Son, however firmly. Thus the church confesses that God the Son was himself conceived when Mary became pregnant—even if theology often labors to evade this confession's

17. Jenson, "Theological Autobiography," 47.
18. Jenson, "Conceptus . . . De Spiritu Sancto," 104.

more alarming entailments. That Mary is The-otokos indeed disrupts the linear time-line or pseudo time-line on which we Westerners automatically—and usually subliminally—locate every event, even the birth of God the Son; but that disruption is all to the theological good.[19]

One other Jensonian christological axiom needs to be noted. Just as surely as Jenson's work is dependent on his understanding of Barth's doctrine of election,[20] it is dependent on his development of Augustine's doctrine of the *totus Christus*. God freely has decided that he would rather not be God at all than to be God without us. And just for that reason, God's history cannot be lived and his story cannot be told without the parts we play in it. There has to be an Israel to be delivered, and a pharaoh for Israel to be delivered from. There have to be "rulers of this present age" to crucify Jesus, and a death for Jesus to be resurrected from. God's sovereign life with us makes a history, and in that history God makes himself real to us, and in that history we become what we're promised to be.

Jenson's Christology has serious pneumatological implications, which we can anticipate here by drawing attention to one defining feature. The Father finds his "I" in the Son, and so does the Spirit: God, after all, is not three I's but one. The Father does not know himself *and* the Son *and* the Spirit. The Father knows himself only *in* the Son *by* the Spirit. The same holds for the Spirit, as well; but of course the Spirit finds himself in Jesus differently than the Father does. The Father knows Jesus as "the Beloved," the

19. Jenson, "Once More the *Logos Asarkos*," 130–31. Jenson means that we must not say, as for example Kathryn Tanner in her *Jesus, Humanity, and the Trinity*, that Jesus is a "version" of the Word.

20. As seen in Jenson, *Alpha and Omega*; and Jenson, *God after God*.

"only-begotten Son," and so knows himself as loving, be-getting Father. The Spirit knows Jesus as the *totus Christus*, and so recognizes himself as the Freedom that exists in the relations of Jesus to the Father and to the members of his community. The Son knows himself as the Father's beloved, as the bearer of the Spirit, and knows us as members of his beloved, Spirit-baptized body. Because he is not ashamed to call us his own, we share his relation to the Father in the Spirit.

Father

God is Father in that God is the *givenness* of reality—both for himself and for us. The "one ultimate fact" is the "mere Fatherhood of God the Father."[21] "The existence of the Father is the ultimate sheer *fact,* the contingency so absolute as to be a necessity."[22] On this front, Jenson is following a dominant tradition in Orthodox theology (as expressed, for example, in John of Damascus's *Expositio fidei*: "We believe in one Father, the beginning and cause of all, begotten of no one, without cause or generation, alone subsisting"). Jenson holds that we can know that God's Fatherhood is ultimate because of what the Scriptures tell us about Jesus's life: he lived and died over against God as the transcendent horizon of his and all other reality. The Jesus narratively described in the Gospels is one who knows himself and everything else only in relation to the Father's will—what already is true because of that will, and what in the end will be true because of that will. Particularly in his prayers, Jesus shows that the Father is the "source of all being that neither we nor yet God himself can get behind, for reasons or for other

---

21. Jenson, "Hidden and Triune God," 9.
22. Jenson, "On Truth and God: 2," 52.

explanations."[23] For creatures, as well as for God himself, there is no getting behind the Father as Father—because the Spirit frees the Father to speak the Word. Circular? Yes, of course. And the circularity is precisely to the point.

According to Jenson, the Father is above all the one who *speaks* and so is spoken to. Creation, for example, is what it is just because it is *commanded* to exist in anticipation of its soon-to-be realized purpose; this commanding is the Father's peculiar contribution to the Triune act of creating.[24] Not only in relation to creation, but also in relation to himself God is a speaker: Jesus, the Word, is nothing but the one the Father "speaks." And precisely by being himself, through the Spirit's gift, the Son makes the Father who he is; the word makes the speaker as surely as the speaker makes the word. This is why, living among us, Jesus reveals the Father no less as he speaks *to* the Father in prayer than when he speaks *for* the Father in teaching and prophecy, in command and promise. The Word, having taken our humanity as his own, calls on the Father from creaturely need—for himself, no doubt, but always also for us—fitting those needs and petitions to the fullness and joy of the divine conversation. In him, then, we see that intercessory prayer is the characteristic human activity. We are never more ourselves than when we are calling on the one who has called us into being for the sake of others.

We might ask if it is necessary to call the first identity of God "Father." But, controversially, Jenson insists that it is. Why? Because the Scriptures present Jesus himself speaking to and about God in this way. No doubt, Jesus did so contingently, within a particular socioreligious context and under peculiar linguistic conditions. Still, we should not

23. Jenson, "Hidden and Triune God," 9.
24. Jenson, "Creation as a Triune Act," 41.

distance ourselves from the practice: to do so would be to take leave of Jesus and so of the faith.

> That Jesus addressed God as "Father" was . . . a matter of using the term of filial address that would in fact pick out the God upon whom he intended to call. Of the possible individuating terms of filial address, "father" rather than "mother" was required, because Jesus' God was the God of Israel. Israel could not, for reasons given in every step of its history with God and still as compelling for Israel as ever, address the Lord as "mother," this being the appropriated address to the principle deity alternative, then as now, to the Lord: the god/ess of fertility religion.[25]

Jenson has been criticized on this point by those (rightly) troubled by patriarchal, misogynistic uses of "Father" language.[26] But he would agree with Sarah Coakley's reading of Aquinas: "Father" is used appropriately only as it names one of the three identities of God. When used to describe an aspect of God's relation to us—that is, when it is used as a metaphor—it is technically inappropriate: no less or more so than other metaphors.[27] In other words, the *name* "Father" is necessary, because it joins us to the truth of Jesus's own life as the Scriptures give it to us. But the *metaphor* "father," while also canonical, is no more or less useful than any other such metaphors. The Father is no more fatherly than he is motherly. The Trinity is no more or less like a parent than he is like a song or a bird or a windstorm. We should not forget that the name has no figurative

25. Jenson, "The Father, He," 104.

26. A misogyny that Jenson names and confronts in *The Triune Identity* and elsewhere.

27. Coakley, *God, Sexuality, and the Self*, 324.

content. It simply points to, singles out, the transcendent source Jesus knew so intimately and makes known to us with that same intimacy. What John Damascene says in his exposition of the Orthodox faith about the notion of procession applies also to the names of the divine relations: "we have learned there is a difference between generation and procession, but the nature of that difference we in no wise understand." "Father," in other words names a difference not only from "Son" and "Spirit" in the divine processions, but also a difference from all analogies, including fatherhood. We have no idea what that difference entails, which is the very reason we must insist upon it.

The Spirit

Jenson's theology is radically christocentric, as even a cursory reading of his work makes plain. But, as already suggested, it is just as thoroughly pneumatological. We might say, in fact, that everything Jenson wants to say about the Father he takes from what he believes about Jesus, and that everything he believes about Jesus comes from what he takes to be true of the Spirit. At the risk of drawing too fine a difference, we might say that for Jenson Jesus is central but the Spirit is primary.

This Spirit-logic comes clearest, perhaps, in Jenson's account of the divine processions. In classical models, the Father begets the Son and breaths the Spirit, and is not himself begotten or breathed. John of Damascus (*Exposito fidei* I.8.), yet again, is exemplary:

> The Father is without cause and unborn, for he is derived from nothing but derives from himself his being. Nor does he derive a single quality from another. Rather, he is himself the beginning and cause of the existence of all things in a

> definite and natural manner. The Son is derived
> from the Father after the manner of generation,
> and the Holy Spirit likewise is derived from the
> Father, yet not after the manner of generation,
> but after that of procession.

Jenson, as we have seen, agrees that the Father is Source, the "ultimate fact" of God's reality and creation's. But, unlike Damascene, Jenson insists that the Father who breathes the Spirit is also freed by the Spirit for that very breathing. On this account, the tradition's description of the divine processions is, in Jenson's judgment, badly malformed. He offers a corrective: of the Trinitarian identities, the Spirit has "metaphysical priority" because, as Scripture says, God *is* Spirit (John 4:24). And drawing on the Augustinian notion of the *nexus amoris*, Jenson argues that precisely because the Spirit is the one who "intends love," the Father and the Son—the two who are the "immediate objects of his intention"—are freed to love each other "with a love that is identical with the Spirit's gift of himself to each of them."[28] God's life, we might say, "moves" from a beginning to an end, an end that makes the beginning possible—indeed, God just is that "movement." Whatever we want to say about the divine attributes applies to that dynamism, that movement, that event. And of the three dynamics of that one movement, the Spirit has primacy in the sense that the Spirit is the fullness of God, the final realization of all God's purposes.

What does this mean for an account of the divine processions? In Jenson's words, "The Father begets the Son and freely breathes the Spirit; the Spirit liberates the Father for the Son and the Son from and for the Father; the Son is

28. Jenson, *Systematic Theology*, 2:158.

begotten and liberated, and so reconciles the Father with the future his Spirit is."[29]

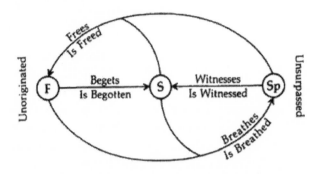

In Jenson's logic, it is precisely as the realization of God's fullness and the final future of creation that the Spirit frees the Father to be the primal beginning as both begetter of the Son and the author of creation. What makes God God is precisely that the divine end and the divine beginning are one, a oneness that is like the oneness of a good story, which is "an ordering by the outcome of the narrated events." A story's "animating spirit" is its power "to liberate each specious present from mere predictabilities, from being the mere consequence of what has gone before, and open it to itself, to itself as what that present is precisely not yet."[30]

THE METAPHYSICS OF GOD'S IDENTITIES

Obviously, for this model to work, there must be some sense in which God's own life is storied and storyable. On Jenson's account, "the dynamism of God's life is a narrative causation

29. Jenson, *Systematic Theology*, 1:161.
30. Jenson, *Systematic Theology*, 2:159.

in and so of God."[31] And talking in that way requires a radical revisioning of what we mean when we speak of God's
attributes. In particular, it requires reworking how we speak
about God's relation to time and to events within time. And
that revisioning of metaphysics is just what Jenson is concerned with doing. His project, at its center, is the attempt
at letting the gospel, and the Scripture's witness to it, set the
terms for Christian metaphysics. In fact, as he sees it, this
has always been the project of the Christian theological tradition, and he aims to think along with that tradition, even
while at points he finds it necessary to critique and rework
aspects of it deeply. He certainly is not interested in simply
re-stating it, but he is equally uninterested in out-and-out
rejection of it.

Eternity & Time

Everyone experiences the passage of time, and sooner or
later we all realize (consciously or not) that that passage
threatens us. We exist at all only insofar as a future remains
open for us. At some point, as time keeps passing, there
will be no more future; everything will have passed into the
past, and we will be no more. Jenson believes that because
of this experience of temporality, and the dread that it gen-
erates, we all need—and so seek out for ourselves—a god
who can give us an "eternity" that transcends time and so
brackets our lives in that transcendence. A god, by Jenson's
definition, is "reality in which the ever-threatening divorce
of past and future is averted, in which what we have been
and what we must or will be somehow rhyme to make a
coherent whole."[32] The real question, therefore, is *how* any

---

31. Jenson, *Systematic Theology*, 2:160.
32. Jenson, "Praying Animal," 312.

particular god transcends time, and what that transcendence means for us as the creatures of that god.

My students usually think of eternity as the kind of time (and heaven as the kind of space) in which God lives. As they imagine it, eternity is more or less temporality without beginning or end. But by Jenson's definition, eternity names the way that a god can be relied on to guarantee survival into one kind of future or another. For our lives to have meaning, we have to have a god to bank on.[33] In the Western tradition, people have tended to imagine gods who remain impervious to time's passing. Think, for example, of Aristotle's First Mover or Plotinus's One. It would be absurd, even blasphemous, to depict these gods as "negotiating with Abraham or dining with Israel's elders." It would be just as absurd to depict humans seeing these gods from behind, as the book of Exodus pictures Moses seeing the God of Israel.[34] Such gods, however magnificent, cannot *communicate* with creatures and so cannot share a history with them, much less make covenant with them. The God of the gospel, however, does communicate and does make covenant with creatures. In Jensonian terms, the transcendence that the gospel reveals is eternal in that it makes sense of our lives by weaving past, present, and future together into a story. The God of the gospel can do this because, as Father, Son, and Spirit, he bounds our existence—and so can bind it into a meaningful whole.

That brings us face-to-face with perhaps Jenson's most controversial claim: God's identity is "set by what he does in time."[35] It is, he says, "the metaphysically fundamental fact of Israel's and the church's faith that its God is freely

33. Here, Jenson's work is resonant with the vision of meaning in George Steiner's *Real Presences*.

34. Jenson, "What Kind of God Can Make a Covenant," 5.

35. Jenson, *Large Catechism,* 8.

but, just so, truly self-identified by, and so with, contingent created temporal events." In particular, the events of *Jesus's* life are determinative—not only for creatures, but also for the Creator. God's reality is determined in what happens with Mary's son. In fact, in Jenson's phrasing, God just is what happens between Jesus and his Father in their Spirit.[36]

> The doctrine of Trinity is at its root the insistence that the history God has with his people, plotted by the relations of its dramatis personae, is not only our life but his. In his history with us, precisely as Israel's Scripture plots it, God is the Author of the story, and a personal Doer and Sufferer within the story, and the Breath of Life that enlivens and binds the two—in Christian jargon, he is Father, Son/Logos and Spirit. The doctrine of Trinity, right to the farthest reaches of its dialectical development, is merely the conceptualized insistence that God is not Father, Son/Logos and Spirit only for us, but for himself.[37]

It is easy to mistake Jenson's meaning. Even otherwise capable theologians—like George Hunsinger and Oliver Crisp, for example—have published uncomfortably bad critiques of Jenson's systematics, largely because they could not make sense of what he wants to say about God's being in relation to creaturely existence.[38] So how are we to understand him? How do we avoid their mistakes?

We need, first, to bear in mind the ways that Jenson uses the language of "person." In Jenson's account, "person" is being used of God in two different senses. In keeping with

36. Jenson, *Systematic Theology,* 1:47.

37. Jenson, "What Kind of God Can Make a Covenant," 18.

38. Hunsinger, "Robert Jenson's Systematic Theology"; Crisp, "Robert Jenson on the Pre-Existence of Christ."

received usage, it refers to what the Father, Son, and Spirit are distinctly in relation to each other. But it also refers to what the Father, Son, and Spirit are inseparably in relation to creation. In the first sense, there are three persons. In the second, there is one.

What is the logic that unites these uses? Jenson argues that all persons, whether the divine one or the human ones, are in fact persons just insofar as their experiences have narrative coherence. What distinguishes the personal from all personal creatures is that God's narrative coherence is identical with himself at every point. In other words, God is who he is just in being faithful to himself. *How* he is both entirely determines and is determined entirely by *who* he is. On this point, Jenson is not far removed from Thomas Aquinas: the divine essence and the divine existence are one. God is God's own reason for existence. God is who he is precisely because he freely decides to be what he is.[39] And in the same way, history is what it is because God, Father, Son, and Spirit, has decided freely to be for us and not against us or without us.

Second, we need to distinguish the notion of person from the notion of identity. We can state it in a formula: because God is *personally* involved in time with created persons, he has a particular *identity*. The nature of temporal existence, at least as Jenson understands it, requires this distinction. A person can enter into conversation and partnership with other persons only insofar as they have a reliable identity. "There are many putative gods and many putative lords . . . the true God tells which one he is."[40]

Jenson holds that unlike the God of Israel, the God whom the church worships, pagan gods have no regard for their identities. Their deity consists precisely in their

39. Jenson, *Canon and Creed,* 92.
40. Jenson, *Large Catechism,* 7.

immunity from time, so they have no need to maintain an identity. Even if initially their worship uses apparently identifying names and descriptions, eventually these names and descriptions, as well as the identities that they serve, are abandoned as worshipers learn to transcend earthly/temporal/bodily restrictions.[41] The God of the Scriptures, however, never transcends his identity. Indeed, in the language of the Pentateuch, he is *jealous* of his identity. He is who he says he is, and he does everything he must to make sure we can trust what he has revealed about himself. This must be so, Jenson believes, for the gospel to be reliably good news. If God transcends his identity, if he is other than who he says he is, if he at any point is other than what he has shown himself to be, then he is finally unidentifiable and the genuine mutuality that the gospel promises is simply impossible.

It is worth lingering over these claims, because they are near the heart of Jenson's theology. As he sees it, God, in creating a history for us and sharing that history with us, is always being faithful to himself, and precisely in that way he both reveals his identity to and effects his identity for himself and for us. Notice: what God does for himself and what God does for us are one and the same. But this is not to say that God is dependent on creation, or that God is somehow altered by creatures into a truer, more beautiful God. It is to say, instead, that God freely decides to be our God, freely determines to be with us rather than without us. We know this is so in the event of incarnation: God makes himself—for himself, and for us—available and identifiable in the Word-made-flesh. Therefore, we know the Father in the same way he knows himself: in the Son.

41. Jenson, *Systematic Theology*, 1:47.

Creation & Change

Does not talking in these ways suggest that God is dependent on creation for his existence and identification? Or that God is changed by his engagements in and with creatures? No. Nothing can keep God from being the God he determines to be for us, and neither creation nor incarnation should be thought to constitute a change of any kind in God. In keeping with these commitments, Jenson again and again insists that God is not made to be God by what creation does to him, but by what he does in history for himself and for us.[42] God is the God he is because of what he does for us, not what we do for him. Creating and the taking up of creatureliness as his own do not make God a different God from what he would have been otherwise—precisely because there is and can be no "otherwise." As Jenson insists, "we must indeed think that God remains himself, come what may in his history with us." But even so, we must not allow ourselves to think God remains faithful to himself by immunity to or relational distance from our reality and us. In fact, as Kathryn Tanner explains, precisely because God is not one being among beings, one agent among other agents, God can be closer to us than we are to ourselves or to each other.[43] In human-to-human interaction, we have always to fear the risks of engagement and influence. But we do not have to fear that from God.

A comparison may help make the point. Maximus insists that God, the Creator of all being, is not a being—and

---

42. See Wright, *Dogmatic Aesthetics,* 102–18. I would only add that what many take for "Hegelianism" in Jenson comes instead from a narrative reading of Israel's scriptures that finds in Israel's eschatological hope the reconciliation of otherwise hopelessly contrasting visions of Israel's calling and destiny. See, for example, Jenson, *Ezekiel,* 238–39.

43. Tanner, *Jesus, Humanity, and the Trinity,* 2–4.

precisely for that reason he cannot be an origin, an intermediary state, or a consummation. God does not cause and is not affected by causes or effects, all of which are creaturely and so fall entirely under the sway of his sovereignty.[44] One might think this contradicts Jenson's account, but in fact the two accounts harmonize beautifully.

> God is the origin, intermediary state and consummation of all created things, but as acting upon things not as acted upon, which is also the case where everything else we call Him is concerned. He is origin as Creator, intermediary state as provident ruler, and consummation as final end. For, as Scripture says, "All things are from Him and through Him, and have Him as their goal" (Rom 11: 36).[45]

With all of this Jenson agrees. He would only add that God acts even in being acted upon. As he has said, God suffers freely, which means that unlike creatures, God does not suffer the fact that he suffers. Therefore, God is in all things as source, guide, and goal by acting (as Creator) even within, as well as without and upon, creation. The Father, acting without time; the Spirit, acting upon time; and the Son, within time, freely acting and being acted upon as a creature in divine communion with the Father in the Spirit. In that ever-active acting-and-being-acted-upon, the Trinity creates, saves, and consummates all things. Even when God is at our mercy, he is merciful.

Contingency & Faithfulness

Talking in this way helps us to see how we can affirm (as Scripture seems to indicate) that God truly is affected by

44. Maximus, *Two Hundred Chapters on Theology* I.4.
45. Ibid., I.10.

what happens with and to us without in any way compromising who or what he is. Assuming humanity as his own, he enters fully into creaturely existence, into the cause-and-effect eventualities of history, so that we experience him as he is in his personal identity. This is necessary for us, because "our only hope is God's personal stake in the good he wills for us."[46] And it is possible for God because Jesus, the Word, is both God and with God as another than God. Just in that Jesus is the Son of the Father through the Spirit it is possible that what happens with him and to him determines the nature of creaturely reality. In Jenson's own words, "the contingency of the world is founded in the contingency of Jesus's life, death, and resurrection . . . [T]he contingently particular story of Jesus is the universal truth of created reality."

> It is because Jesus was truly tempted and so might have fallen, and because the Father was not compelled to raise Jesus from the death to which his steadfastness brought him, and because this contingently faithful and rescued person is the eternal Son for whom all things were created (Col. 1:15–20) that all created being might not have been.[47]

If this seems weirdly speculative and unorthodox, consider what Irenaeus said about the Logos: "Since he who saves already existed, it was necessary that he who would be saved should come into existence, that the one who saves should not exist in vain."[48] Fr. John Behr, commenting on this passage, admits that it might jar modern theological

46. Jenson, *Ezekiel*, 63.

47. Jenson, *Canon and Creed*, 92.

48. *Against Heresies* III.22.3; Jenson depends heavily on Douglas Farrow's reading of Irenaeus's Trinitarian metaphysics. Thanks to Fr. Al Kimel for reminding me of this connection, and for directing me to Fr. John Behr's thoughts on this passage in Irenaeus.

sensibilities. But he insists that Irenaeus's statement is in fact in keeping with the Orthodox tradition, and he lauds him for theologizing "strictly from within the economy, from what can in fact be known and spoken about . . . of God's activity and revelation in Christ."[49] And Behr concludes, with Irenaeus and so, at least in part, with Jenson, that the crucifixion of Jesus grounds the existence of the world.

> Theologically speaking, creation and its history begins with the Passion of Christ and from this "once for all" work looks backwards and forwards to see everything in this light, making everything new. Christian cosmology, elaborated as it must be from the perspective of the Cross, sees the Cross as impregnated in the very structure of creation . . . The power of God revealed in and through the Cross brought creation into being and sustains it in existence . . . Just as the date of the Passion in antiquity was considered to be 25 March (which . . . was the basis for calculating the date of his nativity, nine months later), so also in antiquity 25 March was considered to be the very date of creation, the Creation which revolves around the axis of the eternal, immovable Cross. As paradoxical as it might sound, one can say, theologically, that creation and salvation were effected simultaneously on that day, 25 March, A.D. 33, when Christ gave himself for the life of the world.[50]

For Jenson, then, God is faithful within the contingencies of time. Indeed, faithfulness would be meaningless otherwise. If the incarnation is what the gospel claims it to be, then God does not protect himself from time, but makes commitments in time and remains faithful to them across

49. Behr, *Irenaeus of Lyon*, 146–47.
50. Behr, *Mystery of Christ*, 90–91.

time.[51] Jesus, God the Word, really did present himself to the Patriarchs. He really did write the Ten Words for Moses and Israel. He really did speak through the prophets. He really did take on flesh in the womb of Mary. He really did "mewl and puke on his mother's lap."[52] He really was tempted by Satan in the wilderness. He really was afraid in the garden. He really did die on the cross.[53] If we tell the story any other way, we rob it of its authenticity and immediacy, and therefore strip it of its power to transform us. God, as John Webster reminds us, is the holy one *in our midst*. God shares a history with us, lives in this present with us, finds himself in our reality just so that we might find ourselves in his—without in any way losing himself to the ravages of time or the powers of sin and death. God triunely makes himself invulnerably vulnerable to contingencies in order to save creation from death by means of those very contingencies. Through it all, in it all, God is truly with us, sharing our history with us and allowing us to share his. And, as Jenson would have it, only a thrice-holy God could do something so strange. Because the Father wills it so and because the Spirit brings it to completion, the Son is free to enter fully into our history, assuming our humanity, submitting to our history's realities—even to the humiliation of torture and execution and the horror of death.

God is not made to be other than he is by this share in our history. For all the ways that he wants to qualify it, Jenson affirms the notion of God's *impassibility*: "God is indeed impassible in the sense that external events cannot alter his personal identity or character." And he also affirms divine *simplicity*, so long as we do not allow it to subvert the

51. Jenson, *Systematic Theology*, 2:217.
52. One of Jenson's favorite bits from Luther.
53. Jenson, *Song of Songs*, 77.

doctrine of the Trinity.[54] And he also affirms divine *aseity* and *immutability*, so long as these notions do not tempt us to think that God is securely removed from the happenings of our history, disengaged from us and our lives. God is (truly!) with us. "God is not eternal in that he adamantly remains as he began, but in that he always creatively opens to what he will be; not in that he hangs on, but in that he gives and receives; not in that he perfectly persists, but in that he perfectly anticipates."[55]

Anticipation & Existence

Because God's being is event, his identity is grounded not in persistence against the changes of time (as found in pagan philosophies) but (as the logic of the gospel requires) in anticipation of the fullness of time. In Jenson's own formulation, "Since the Lord's self-identity is constituted in dramatic coherence, it is established not from the beginning but from the end, not at birth but at death, not in *persistence* but in *anticipation*."[56] Even for God, "the future is not the present, yet it has presence."[57] But what sense does this make? Why does Jenson want to insist that the gospel calls for thinking in these terms? It seems he is convinced that to be human is, above all, to live in time, to be caught up in the movement from past to future through a present that exerts irresistible pressure on us. We *must* make sense of our lives as a whole, one way or another, somehow knitting our future to our past in a present-tense storied account. The promise of the gospel is that God does in fact make sense of our lives, and that he can do so because he is before

54. Jenson, *Song of Songs*, 46.

55. Jenson, *Systematic Theology*, 1:217.

56. Ibid., 1:66 (italics original).

57. Jenson, *Ezekiel*, 87.

our past and after our future, and just in that way present to us in our present.

Jenson's language is no doubt eccentric, but what he wants to articulate is perhaps not that unfamiliar to us if we hear it in other terms. Take, for example, these reflections from one of my students:

> God's kingdom was, is, and is coming. His king-
> dom is no less his kingdom in the beginning
> than it is in the end . . . He is the king in the
> prophets, the king in the new and living way,
> and the king in the kingdom coming . . . So, is
> the kingdom really something that is not yet?
> Maybe historically, in the king we are already
> there. His testimony is the spirit of prophecy.[58]

The point, at least as I take it, is relatively straightforward: the kingdom is the realization of God's will in fullness, and for God that fullness is always already there. But not in a way that leaves God in stasis. God's life is lively, dynamic, dramatic. But it moves changelessly, from fullness to fullness.

The key, at least from a Jensonian perspective, is in that last line of my student's comment: God is the God of *prophecy*, a God who speaks to us from the eschatological past about an eschatological future that for us no less than for the first hearers is our present. Prophecy, in other words, is not about historical prediction, but about an anticipation in history of the coming of God in eschatological fullness. In our present, whenever that is, the triune God comes at us from all directions. If we go forward, anticipating the future, he is there; if we go backward, remembering the past, he is present; if we turn to the left hand, or to the right, he is both arriving and already arrived.

58. It was a comment made in a journal reflection; there was no topic assigned or title. It was submitted in January 2015.

2

TRUTH

Method & Meaning

In the opening of his *Systematics*, Jenson devotes relatively little attention to methodology, holding that his theological commitments prohibit lengthy prolegomena. But this in fact belies how critical theological method is to him and his work. As he himself acknowledges, from his earliest work to his last, he is at every turn concerned with getting the gospel said at a particular time in a way that performs for its speakers and hearers what it promises. But he is concerned also with doing theology in a way that can be translated beyond his own time and place. As a result, his approach is every bit as constructive methodologically as it is revisionary theologically, and he has as much to teach us about how to think as about what and why to believe.

At the heart of Jenson's theological method is a conviction about the truth and its relation to God as dramatic event, a conviction that owes much to Jenson's reading of Thomas Aquinas. Early in his *Summa Theologiae*, Saint

Thomas asks whether or not God is personally to be regarded as the truth. And he answers that not only is truth to be found in God, but that God himself is to be regarded as "supreme and primary truth." "God" and "truth" ultimately name the same reality, although of course they do so in distinct registers. This must be so, Jenson concludes, because as Saint Thomas makes clear, only in God is the relationship of true propositions and true realities perfectly at-one-ed: "not only is his being conformed to his thought of himself, but his being is identical with his act of thus knowing himself."[1] God is the truth of truth, the reality that makes truth true.

HOW GOD IS THE TRUTH

Many, if not most, of Jenson's deepest and most central theological convictions came to him early in his career—as this one certainly did. In an essay published in 1961, when Jenson was teaching at Luther College, he writes, "the truth is God-revealing-himself, God-present-to-me, *deus loquens*. Truth, that is, *occurs*. It occurs when God interrupts my flight from him and places himself in my way as the unavoidably decisive pole of my life. Truth is Jesus."[2] More than forty years later, while leading the Center for Theological Inquiry, he makes more or less exactly the same claim: "God *is* knowing, or as we are more likely to say, truth. Thus Godhead as truth is founded in intersubjectivity, precisely as he is as love. In God, therefore, that reality is known and reality is loved are aspects of the one fact of the triune intersubjectivity."[3]

1. Jenson, "On Truth and God: 1," 387.
2. Jenson, "Liberating Truth and Liberal Education," 213.
3. Jenson, *On Thinking the Human*, 54.

Jenson being Jenson, of course, he has to work out the movements of that intersubjectivity across the triune processions. So, unlike Saint Thomas, who considers the truth as existing either in the mind (*in intellectu*) or in things (*in re*), Jenson holds that truth's "decisive location" is in speech (*in sermone*).[4] Analogy to the doctrine of the Trinity is ready at hand; the Father does not merely think; the Father speaks. And what he speaks is the Son who is his "Word." And the Word, according to Scripture, is not mere Logos but Jesus, showing that the truth is not mere rationality, but "mutual communication"—just as the Gospel stories about Jesus's life suggest. The Spirit is the freedom that makes it so the Father and Son are free to love each other freely, keeping either from making the other a mere object, and so enslaving and demeaning one another.

> The God of the gospel is eternally in actual converse within himself, is eternally *sermo*. And this discourse is the truth itself because it is the very being of God, in whom—just as Thomas worked it out—*Veritas in intellectu* and *Veritas in re* are not distinct. In general, speech is the link between intellect and the things intellect knows and wills; thus actual speech is the home of *veritas*, first in God and thereupon in us.[5]

HOW THE TRUTH HAPPENS TO US

In this light, it is easy to see why Jenson regards lively conversation as "the first home of truth."[6] On his view, this lively conversation is foundationally intra-Trinitarian:

4. Jenson, "On Truth and God: 2," 51.

5. Ibid., 54.

6. Jenson, *Conversations with Poppi about God*, 10.

God-to-God. Then, derivatively, it is conversation extra-Trinitarianly: God the Trinity, "speaks" to us, to me. And that is how the truth is known: God speaks and by speaking awakens response-ability.

When Jenson describes God as speaking he means exactly that. As the Gospels reveal, the Father speaks to the Son and about him: "In Mark's account of Jesus's baptism, the Father addresses him as his Son, and indeed this address seems to *be* the Father's eternal begetting; Matthew and Luke then report that bystanders heard the address." And what happens in the history of Jesus is what is happening in the drama of the divine life: John 17 records an entire speech of the Son to the Father, which is intended to be overheard by the disciples, and John 12:27–28 is an actual dialogue between the Son and his Father, also for the sake of those who will overhear it. Jenson insists we must not interpret these exchanges as events only in the life of the "economic" Trinity, "for the obtrusively incarnate speaker in John directly identifies himself as the Word who antedates Abraham, and prays for the glory he had with the Father before creation."[7]

The truth must happen to us. And it must happen in ways that free us to interact, to respond, to engage with God and with one another. And because God is the truth, the truth happens only as God happens: "grace" is just another way of naming the activity of the Spirit in our lives. Therefore, conversation, the lively exchange of truth-in-love, is quite literally everything. We exist at all only because we are addressed eternally by God, and we come into the fullness of life just as we respond in time to God by addressing one another lovingly and truthfully. As Jenson contends, I am myself only by God's intrusions—the "hey, you!" or "hold

7. Jenson, "On Truth and God: 2," 52.

it!" that he speaks so that I may transcend myself entirely in the freedom given to engage God and neighbor lovingly.

THE END OF THEOLOGY

The work of theology, then, is always in service of the gospel by which God addresses us. As Jenson often said, theology is "maintenance of a message," which precisely to be itself can never be spoken or heard the same way twice. The gospel, if it is truly the Word of God, performs what it promises and enacts what it declares. But if the human speaking of that Word is to be faithful, it must identify God rightly and articulate the gospel clearly. The work of theology is the work of finding the articulation of the gospel for a particular time and place that identifies God rightly for the people of that time and place so that they can hear the Word that calls them to life.

Early in his career, before he had finished the PhD, Jenson found himself agreeing with Bultmann: faith is openness to the future. But a question nagged him: what is the *content* of that future? Bultmann, he was convinced, had no good answer to the question, and so was contending for a groundless and objectless faith—or, worse, a self-grounded and self-desired faith. Departing from Bultmann, therefore, Jenson works to *describe* the future that the gospel opens, convinced that only insofar as such a description is made is it possible to talk faithfully about faith.[8] In turn, he came to see that the work of theology is the work of shaping that description so that it is as true, as sound, as is possible.

8. Jenson, "Theological Autobiography," 48.

The Truth and Philosophy

Kate Sonderegger, among others, finds Jenson's work too revisionist, too dismissive of the classical metaphysical tradition. Among other things, she faults him for rejecting Hellenistic philosophy and its place in Christian dogmatics. But in truth, he does not reject it tout court, even though he thinks the patristic project of gospelizing Hellenism is an ongoing, unfinished project, and that not every culture and people needs to accept Greek philosophical frames of reference in order to believe the gospel faithfully. His vision is near to Staniloae's:

> In Christianity, there are two conceptions of God, one which comes from the Bible and which belongs to Christian life and experience, and the other which comes from Greek philosophy. The first presents God as the living God, full of concern and interest for humankind. The second presents God as unmoved and immoveable. Eastern Orthodoxy has made a great effort to combine and harmonise the two conceptions. It has sought to reconcile both these ways of thinking about God.[9]

Jenson differs from Staniloae in that he is less concerned with *harmonizing* Scripture and the Greek metaphysics of timelessness than with *revising* the Hellenistic tradition in ways that better fit the ontology suggested in the scriptural metanarrative. But he does not want to replace the tradition or eradicate it altogether; indeed, he thinks that for Christians formed in the Western tradition, the concepts and language of Hellenistic philosophy are now a necessary part of witness to the gospel (as it would

9. Staniloae, *Eternity and Time*, 6.

not be for Christians formed in Eastern traditions, or for Jews or Muslims).[10]

The Truth and the Scriptures

Jenson believes that theology accomplishes its end, generation after generation, in various missionary contexts, only as it reads the Scriptures in conversation with the Christian dogmatic tradition. In the Spirit's wisdom, canon—"the total narrative by which Scripture identifies God"[11]—and creed are "matched puzzle pieces," and only as they are matched rightly can theology find the language necessary to describe the future faith desires and claims as its own.

Jenson's "Nicene theory" of interpretation is concerned with discerning the "christological plain sense." And it does so on the presumption that "both the biblical text and the church's trinitarian and christological teachings are *true*."[12] On this point Peter Leithart gets Jenson exactly right:

> Scripture plays a generative as well as a regulative role in theology. And for Jenson, these two operations go together: The oddities of the Bible's narrative of God and his ways with creation give rise to puzzles to which Jenson offers conceptual solution, but those solutions must in turn be coherent with the Bible's narrative. All of Jenson's characteristic novelties—the peculiarities of his Trinitarian thought, his denial of the *logos asarkos*, his construal of beginning and end, of protology and eschatology—arise from

10. See Jenson, "Toward a Christian Theology of Israel," 43–56; and Jenson, "The Risen Prophet," 57–67.

11. Jenson, *Systematic Theology*, 1:46.

12. Jenson, *Ezekiel*, 24.

his attempts to make theological, analytical, and metaphysical sense of Scripture.[13]

As Leithart makes clear, Jenson refuses the standard moves of "classical theism" because they essentially treat "the biblical God" as nothing more than an anthropomorphic analog to the real God. Against those habits, Jenson aims to turn "the specifics of the Bible into a critique of the presumed fundamental theology."[14]

Jenson's commentary work (on Song of Songs and Ezekiel) shows that he is trained as a modern interpreter. But his hermeneutics finally has more in common with precritical exegesis: he is concerned above all with the theological import of the text as it is given to us. So, for example, when he reads about the divine self-disclosure at Sinai, he acknowledges he is aware that Exodus's description "can be picked apart into sources, and all interesting tensions thus removed." But this, he insists, is completely beside the theological point. And when he reads Ezekiel's vision of the throne, he asks why the one envisioned looks like a man, and answers: "because the second person of the Trinity *is* a man—Jesus of Nazareth."[15] Finally, when reading the description of God's passions in Song of Songs, he concludes: "No part of Scripture makes sense if our reading is controlled by the dogma that to be God is simply to be without passion, and the theological allegory solicited by the Song least of all."[16]

As I have said, most of Jenson's theological commitments took shape early in his career, but not so his view of the Scripture's inspiration. Throughout the bulk of his

13. Leithart, "Jenson as Theological Interpreter," 46.

14. Ibid.

15. Jenson, *Ezekiel*, 42–43.

16. Jenson, *Song of Songs*, 77.

work, he assumes that a doctrine of inspiration is unnecessary, if not also impossible. But eventually he came to see that only by the Spirit's intervention can Scripture be what the gospel suggests it is: prophetic narrative and narratival prophecy. How does this inspiration work? First, by the Spirit's guidance of events determined by God to be told for the good of God's people through time. Then, by bringing to speech God's Word so that a specific plot to history becomes recognizable. And, finally, by the Spirit's guidance of the writing down and preservation of these writings in a way that makes a whole narrative.[17]

THE BEGINNING OF THEOLOGY

Jenson discovered the need for theology early in his studies. He recalls coming to Luther Seminary "well fitted in most ways but one": he was not sure he *really* believed the gospel, as he thought he had to do. Given that he intended to invest his life in the ministry, and because his mind was soaked in reading Kierkegaard, he found the problem overwhelming. Then, while researching for a paper, he found in the writings of Carl Rosenius, the Swedish Lutheran, the argument that "sin" is the same as unbelief in the forgiveness the gospel promises. In that moment, the importance—the indispensability—of theological work hit him with force: "It was a fundamental liberation; a step of theological argument let a word of 'gospel' be said where before there had only been 'law.' I have been convinced of the necessity of theology ever since, and with a consistent purpose."[18]

Rowan Williams has remarked that a theologian must be prepared to speak both for and to a particular ecclesial tradition. If they cannot do both equally well, then they

17. Jenson, *On the Inspiration of Scripture*, 53–54.
18. Jenson, "About Dialog, and the Church," 38.

cannot serve the church as a whole. For his part, Jenson is a recognizable Lutheran theologian. Much of his career was spent training Lutheran ministers and shaping official Lutheran intra- and extra-denominational dialogues. But he is clear that he was called to think and to write *for* the church catholic: "theology must be written for the undivided church that the Spirit will surely someday grant."[19] Any other theology runs the risk of impeding the Spirit's work.

Jenson, of course, is postmodern enough to realize that theology is always done in a specific context for particular people. His own project is self-consciously done for and offered to a late-modern, pluralistic audience in the Western cultural tradition, which is why he finds it necessary to begin his christological reflections and constructions not with "human nature" or "the historical Jesus" but with "narrative," by which he means, "a set of temporally distinguishable events whose togetherness to the set is determined as follows: each successive item, except the first one, must be dramatically appropriate to the preceding one, and every successive item, except the latter, must be dramatically open."[20] From this point, Jenson can take "Jesus in Israel" as a narrative, and then conclude:

> When it is told in any sort, and when the real hopes and fears of those who speak respectively are discussed at the same time, and when the two manners of speaking mutually interpret themselves, the gospel takes place. Or else, gospel happens in so far as this mutual interpretation becomes effective in a certain way; that is to say, in so far as an appellation occurs which

19. Jenson, "Theological Autobiography," 54.
20. Jenson, "Aspekte der Christologie," 114.

attributes a new temporal structure to those who are addressed.[21]

Jenson knows that because it is context-specific, no theology can be translated whole cloth into another context. Hence, people will have to make what they can of his project, adapting it as they can in attempts to maintain the message of the gospel in their time and place. Theologians, he says, do what they can to serve the church, trusting the Holy Spirit to make of their work something more than they could possibly intend or dare to hope for themselves. Their work is like bread cast on the waters; if others find it, and are fed by it, then God is to be praised.

Finally, given Jenson's emphasis on dialog and conversation, it is fitting that so much of his work was birthed out of deep theological friendships—perhaps especially with Carl Braaten; with his granddaughter, Solveig; and with his wife, Blanche, whom he insisted deserved coauthor credit on all of his works. On numerous occasions, Jenson praised his most famous teacher, Karl Barth, for the respect he showed his students—the greatness of the man somehow indicated by the graciousness with which he engaged those who came to learn from him. From my own experiences with Jens (as he invited us to call him), I have come to see that he too was a theologian whose work not only coheres systematically, but also cohered personally—he lived the life of faith he described, and all of us are the richer for it.

21. Ibid.

3

CREATION

Being as Communion

The story of Scripture opens with a straightforward dog-matic claim: "In the beginning God created."[1] This claim binds us to confess that God is Creator. But what does the confession actually mean? And how are we to make that confession faithfully in our various times and places? Jen-son insists that faithful confession is possible only as we remember *who* it is that creates and *why* he does so. Who creates? The triune God revealed by the gospel. Why does he create? Because he delights in what is other than himself. As Jenson says to his granddaughter, Solveig, "All the plan-ets, galaxies, stars, animals, black holes . . . God's excited by it. He wouldn't have done it if he were not interested in it."[2] God opens his life joyfully to include us so that we might live, move, and have our being precisely in that joy, which is our strength.

1. Jenson, "Aspects of a Doctrine of Creation," 17.
2. Jenson, *Conversations with Poppi about God*, 43.

THE TIME GOD HAS FOR US

Jenson's doctrine of creation begins, ends, and is carried along by his revisionist understanding of time. Or, more precisely, it is carried along by his revisionist understanding of God's relation to us, which makes time what it is. Following Barth, he finds that the Christian theological tradition wrongly posits eternity as opposed to time—as if God is bracketed out of our lives by time, existing beginninglessly and endlessly beyond the edges of our reality. But Scripture, Jenson insists, requires us to think the relation of eternity and time as analogous instead of dichotomous. God's life is eternal precisely in that it brackets us *in* time. Or, to say the same thing another way, eternity names how God is with us in time so that our beginning and our end cohere as one story. Because God is a communion, a lively and dramatic conversation, it is, Jenson contends, "sort of natural" (but only sort of!) that God creates. In a word, then, we are made *for* communion with God *by* the communion of God, and we exist just as God makes time for us and we take time for him. This is the heart of Jenson's doctrine of creation.

The Time God Has for Himself

"God creates by taking time within his eternal time for others than the three who are himself." In making this claim, Jenson is not suggesting that God is subject to time, of course. But he is saying that God is the subject of time—affording temporality its being, its dynamism, its meaning. Christian dogma requires us to confess that God is not in time as we are; but Jenson wants to add that time is truly in God, fitted to the reality of the divine life and just in that way constructed as a fitting home for us.

Because God takes time for us within the timeliness of his own life, he shares a history with us. And he shares that history with us in such a way that history has not only a source but also a direction and a fulfillment. We might say it like this: the Trinity lives, moves, and has being; therefore, time can move. Time can move; therefore, we can live, move, and have our being from, in, and toward God. God moves in his being from fullness to fullness; indeed, as Trinity, he fulfills and is fulfilled as fullness. Precisely in these movements, we are created, redeemed, and glorified in God as our beginning, our aim, and our end.

We can perhaps get a better grasp of Jenson's account of God's "time" if we compare it with Dumitru Staniloae's view of time's relation to eternity. Staniloae, like Jenson, holds that time and eternity cannot be simply opposed. If we are to think of God personally, as Scripture declares we must, then we cannot imagine eternity as anything but "a fullness of life . . . the perfect communion which subsists between eternal Persons whose love is inexhaustible."[3]

> Time is not a sin against eternity, a fall from eternity, something opposed to it. The eternity of God, as life in its plenitude, as an eternal and perfect love between the Persons who are perfectly in union with one another, carries within itself the possibility of time. Time, on the other hand, carries within itself the possibility of eternity which can be realized in communion with God by his grace; for God can enter into a relationship of love with temporal beings.

With all of this Jenson obviously agrees. But he does differ from Staniloae on at least one critical point: for Staniloae, time is *interval,* and an interval is necessarily a failure of response to love. As he puts it, "Love is the gift of oneself to another, and the waiting for the full return of that gift from the other in response. Only in a complete and

3. Staniloae, *Eternity and Time,* 7.

immediate response to the offer of love is love fully realised." The name of that interval in response is "time" and "as such, [it] represents a spiritual distance between persons." Time, therefore, cannot exist for God because God's life is love fully realized, love without even the shadow of "spiritual distance."

Obviously, Jenson would agree that there is no failure of love in God. But he would not accept that an interval in response is necessarily a failure or shortcoming. "Time" is eventfulness, and the interval—the silence between the notes, so to speak—is not failure, but the structure of the event. Anyway, that is what the resurrection of Jesus suggests: Holy Saturday is not a failure within the divine life but the fullness of God's communion encompassing even the depths of hell.

Time, Narrative, and Self-Understanding

To make sense of our lives, at least as a whole, as a history, we have to think narratively. The literary theorist Jonathan Culler explains: "The model for historical explanation is . . . the logic of stories: the way a story shows how something came to happen."[4] Jenson is convinced that this is so because the God who makes time is himself a dramatic event that "moves" not from less to more or better to best, but from fullness to fullness, from glory to glory. Hence, the very characteristics of temporal experience—its dramatic movement, its irreversibility, its tripartite structure—reveal something to us both about the God who makes time for us and about what we ourselves are as creatures of this peculiar God.

4. Culler, *Literary Theory*, 19.

The Creator/Creature Distinction

More than a few critics—some charitable and others anything but—have complained that Jenson blurs the distinction between Creator and creature by his revisioning of
God's relation to time. They take him to mean that God is
changed by creation, made into a different God over time
by what he does in time. But of course Jenson means no
such thing. As he maintains at every turn, there is God and
there is everything else. "Before there is the creature, there
is God and nothing. And this nothing is not the kind that
can be the antecedent of something. God and only God is
the creature's antecedent."[5] And like Aquinas and others
in the dogmatic tradition, he holds that "everything else"
is there at all only because God, who is beyond existence,
freely decides that it should be so. He also agrees with
Rahner, although he would surely phrase it differently: "We
and the existents of our world really and truly are different
from God not in spite of, but because we are established
in being by God."[6] And he agrees with Kathryn Tanner as
well: "Relations with God are utterly non-competitive because God, from beyond this plane of created reality, brings
about the *whole* plane of creaturely being and activity in his
goodness."[7]

   Truth be told, Jenson's affirmation of the Creator/
creation distinction could hardly be more forcefully stated.
He goes so far as to insist that even "transcendence" cannot
accurately explain the Creator's difference,[8] because God's
otherness from creation is not analogous to *any* reality, and

5. Jenson, "Aspects of the Doctrine of Creation," 22.

6. Rahner, *Foundations of the Christian Faith*, 79.

7. Tanner, *Jesus, Humanity, and the Trinity*, 4.

8. Here, Jenson's use of the term differs from, say, Kathryn Tanner's.
She would agree that God's relation to creation is noncompetitive.

for that very reason is not something God has to safeguard or secure. Human beings transcend the rest of creation by reason of their share in the image of God. God, however, does not transcend creation. As Maximus would say it, God is beyond all creaturely relations, and therefore absolutely without comparison. For example, we should not say that God is wiser than human beings. No, God is the Creator of wisdom itself, so his wisdom cannot but seem like so much foolishness to us, and only by being caught up in his folly are we made truly wise. And the same goes for all the divine attributes.

In Jenson's account, then, the Creator/creature difference is one that God makes just by being God. Specifically, in his own words, it is one that "God enforces by taking action."[9] But we must take pains to be as clear as possible: this "taking action" does not mark a change in God. This is so for two reasons: first, as Aquinas makes clear, unless there is a creation, there is nothing for any change to happen *to*; second, God, simply by being himself for creation, necessarily, inevitably enacts the "infinite qualitative distinction" between God and what he has made.

God enacts the difference between himself and creation especially in the event of *incarnation*, which realizes for us what God determines himself to be. Taking up creatureliness as his own, assuming humanity to himself, God ensures once and for all that there is a difference between himself and creation—and that that difference is perfectly good for us. In Jesus, the divine and the human, the Creatorly and the creaturely, are at-one-ed—and exactly so the difference between God and creation is effected. In the language of Chalcedon, it is precisely because the Creator and creature are inseparably joined in Christ that they are also not confused or altered in any way. Jesus, the Word, is

9. Jenson, "Creator and Creature," 219.

the truth for God as well as for us. God is God in Christ. Creation is creation in Christ. In the language of Saint Paul, precisely because the fullness of God dwells in Christ, he holds all things together.

The Movements of Time and the Movements of God

Jenson formulates his doctrine by following Barth's path-breaking insight: God's eternity is different from time only in that there is perfect peace between source, movement, and goal (not in that there is no movement at all).[10] In this way, creaturely time is regarded as a time within the eternal "time" of the divine life, "a 'distention' in the life that is God and just so the . . . horizon of all events that are not God."[11] And this distention, this making room, makes it so that creatures can exist in the integrity given to them without being absorbed into or undone by the gravity of the divine life. Although Jenson himself never uses this image, we might say that creation is possible because God fasts from himself "in a gift of unconditional hospitality."[12] Or, to come closer to Jenson's usual way of talking, we might say that God creates so that there will be others to share in the feast that is his life.

Typically, my students picture the relation of God, eternity, and time something along these lines: in Eternity Past, the Trinity, conceived as three individual centers of consciousness, foresaw how time would work out as creatures abused their freedom, and recognized the need for some means of salvation first to be accomplished for and

10. For one recent example of Jenson's use of this insight, see Jenson, *Ezekiel*, 87.

11. Jenson, *Systematic Theology*, 2:35.

12. Augustine, "Creation as Perichoretic Trinitarian Conversation," 101.

then to be offered to those who would respond faithfully. After creating, God has remained mainly withdrawn and observing, only occasionally intervening in time to make sure that what has been foreseen and predetermined does in fact take place. Particularly in the incarnation, and especially in the events of Good Friday and Resurrection Sunday, God became more fully involved, sending his Son to die and raising him from the dead as the necessary means of salvation. In the time since Jesus's death and resurrection, all those who believe in Jesus are saved, and are immediately joined in the work of helping others find that same salvation as well. Now, everyone awaits the end of time when Jesus "comes back," initiating Eternity Future with the event of Last Judgment, sorting the "sheep" and "goats" into their respective destinies in heaven and hell.

Needless to say, Jenson rejects this model—even its sophisticated versions. First, as we have already seen, he holds that God is conditioned by nothing except God; therefore, "eternity" does nothing more or less than identify the way that the living God relates to us in the time he has made for us. Eternity and time, therefore, are not antithetically related to one another—not any more than divinity and humanity are. Once this is understood, there is no need to posit an Eternity Past that (temporally?) precedes time, or an Eternity Future that (temporally?) succeeds it. And by doing away with that dual time line, we find ourselves freed up to reimagine what it means for God to act in and upon creation.

As Jenson sees it, we must find a way to say that God, in his fullness, is presently *with* us—he shares our "now." Indeed, God is wherever God is at work, and it is only because God is at work that we have a now at all. The God who is with us and at work upon us is the eternal and triune God—the God who not only foreknows and predestines but who also *postknows* and *postdestines*, knowing us and acting for us as the beginning and as the end, and just in that way giving us the time we need to be the creatures we are called to be.

Providence & Election: How Time is Good for Us

Time, at least in Jenson's description, is the deepest creaturely reality, the creature's most basic created condition. Space and matter, after all, must be present to matter for us. And, of course, the same holds for other people as well. And it holds even for God. If "time is the means by which we conceptualize our locatedness among other people,"[13] then even God must be present for us to commune with him. In fact, to trust in God is to trust that he will be present whenever we truly need him, and that he will make it so that what we experience in the present is finally good for us.

Whatever else it might mean, to say that God is faithful is to say that his care for us is *timely*. In Knight's words, God does not give us people—or any other creatures—faster than we can receive them.[14] God gives *what* we need just *when* we need it.

As we have already noted, Jenson agrees with long-accepted Christian wisdom: time has a dramatic movement from a source toward an end along a meaningful line of development.[15] Time, in other words, is to be regarded as historical. It can be narrated as a story—or it will be so narratable when all is said and done. What is more, that move-

13. Knight, "Time and Persons in the Economy of God," 131

14. Ibid.

15. Many readers sense a Hegelianism lurking behind these claims, but as Wright (*Dogmatic Aesthetics*, 116) makes clear, "Hegel does influence Jenson—in so much as Hegel depicts history as having direction and sense—[but] he neither determines Jenson's Christology nor causes Jenson to collapse the finite into the infinite."

ment is both irreversible and tripartite. Creaturely existence in time is a movement from the past through the present into the future, which of course first becomes the present and then turns into the past. As a result of this irreversible movement, the past as past always lies unalterably behind us, closed to our powers, inaccessible to us except in the imaginations of memory. And the future as future always lies before us, open to various potential realizations, unreal except in the imaginations of anticipation. As Moltmann says, "the future becomes the past, but the past cannot become the future again . . . Whatever is future is *possible*, whatever is present is *real*, and whatever is past is *necessary* because it is unchangeable."[16]

As Jenson reads them, time's three arrows—and the necessity, contingency, and reality they bespeak—point beyond themselves to the dramatic, tripartite life of the God who is their Creator. God is the one who makes the possible possible, the necessary necessary, and the real real because God is the source, guide, and goal of our past, present, and future. And God makes all this so precisely because that is what we need in order to be the creatures he calls us to be, creatures made for communion with him and with all things in him. Time has triune structure and inexorable movement so we might be made over time into creatures apt for full communion with one another and with God.

In such a construal, time itself remains even after the fall a gift, a good, at least structurally. Playing fast and loose with Heideggarian terms, we might say that time is *ontologically* untouched by sin, even while *ontically* it is corrupted by the twisting of our memory, our anticipation, and our presence to one another and to God.[17] How can

16. Moltmann, "What is Time?," 31

17. This is not far from Aquinas's view of what happens to human nature in the fall.

this be so? Because time, ontologically speaking, is nothing other than the divine energies making being possible for us. Or, to rephrase, God determines what time is by how he is present for us, and for obvious reasons sin and death cannot alter that determination. But so long as we remain estranged from God and from our true selves, so long as we are enslaved to sin, so long as death is at work in us, we cannot receive that determination graciously. Salvation, then, names how God works to refit us to time, remaking and then conforming our being to his image so we are apt to receive the gift that time is for us.

Borrowing from Jonathan Edwards, Jenson's metaphysics, at its roots, depends on a deceptively simple claim: "what is real is real because Love loves it."[18] Creatures have no "substance" except God's "grasp" of them.[19] Reality, essentially, is nothing but God's attention given to what is other than God. And because that God is triune as Father, Son, and Spirit, that attention envelops us as a love that is eternally before all things and after all things, always delivering us from nothingness, calling us into deeper and deeper communion with one another. And, in turn, if the gospel is true, we grasp the reality that grasps us just in the eucharistic celebration where we (sharing with God and with one another the creatures of bread and wine) are brought as close as possible in this life to the fullness of the purpose we share with Christ.[20]

In one of his centuries on love, Maximus says that time has "three divisions," and that faith belongs to all three (past, present, future), hope to one (future), and love with the other two (past, present). Why does love not belong to all three? Because the future has no reality for us: we cannot

18. Jenson, *On Thinking the Human*, 53.

19. Ibid., 54.

20. Ibid., 57.

love what is not. The same does not hold for God, however. God has neither faith nor hope, because God is not subject to time as we are but is its creator, guide, and consummator. So, to say that God is love is to say that God loves us before, during, and after everything that happens to us. That is, at least in part, what it means to say that God *is* love. In Jenson's own words,

> God's eternity is not that for him everything is already past, but that in love everything is still open, including the past. His eternity is that he can never be surpassed, never caught up with. He anticipates the future in the sense that however we press forward in time, we always find that God has already been there and is now ahead calling us on.[21]

Theodicy and Theosis: How Time Makes a History

Because God's love is triply harmonious, like a fugue, the time God makes for us makes a history. Or, again, it *will* make a history when God's will is finally done on earth as it already is in heaven where Christ, risen from among the dead, is reckoned as Lord. For now, however, the coherent story of creation cannot be told. Or, better, it cannot be told as *gospel* but only as *law*—except insofar as we read creation's history "by faith and not by sight."

As things currently stand in our world, salvation and damnation, both God's Yes and God's No, are enacted both-at-once; therefore, "[history's] very essence is self-contradiction." Creation, caught in the agonized conflicts of law and grace, death and life, sin and righteousness, shame and peace, remains "irreducibly ambiguous and at odds

21. Jenson, *God after God,* 171.

with itself."[22] Whatever we might want to think, the arc of history does *not* bend toward justice. If, then, history is to end in justice, it must be bent to that shape. History, like we ourselves, must be justified by grace. And this can happen only as the final realization of the Father's bespeaking of reality for us in Christ's actions within time and the Spirit's actions upon it. Only so may what has already happened to Jesus happen to everyone and everything. That is, creation is justified only eschatologically.

The world as we know it—the world as it now stands, short of its eschatological transformation—is constituted by violence and death. This is true of the physical universe, as well as the political, social, and cultural/religious realities that make up its history. All creatures, and all the histories we might tell of creation as a whole or in part, are at this point like Israel's David: hopelessly stained with blood. And, for some reason that we simply cannot fathom, God intends it to be so—or so Jenson, like Luther, believes. Evil and sin, violence and death, wickedness and corruption have been intended by God—although *only* so that Christ might triumph over them for us.[23]

Be that as it may, until God's will is realized entirely, God remains *involved* in the violence of history. God, Scripture says, is "a man of war" (Exod 15:3). And Jenson concludes that it must be so: "had the Lord not fought for—and against—his people of Israel, he could have had no people within actual history, and so no Christ of that people and so no church of that Christ."[24] "God does not rule only from without the rough and tumble of history but also from within it."[25]

22. Jenson, *On Knowledge of Things Hoped For,* 233.

23. Jenson, *Systematic Theology,* 1:73.

24. Jenson, *Ezekiel,* 76.

25. Ibid., 49.

But so long as God is involved in the violence of history, we cannot tell how he is or is not complicit in that violence. As Jenson himself admits,

> It must be acknowledged: God's continuing involvement in the violence of history is indeed a reason to turn one's back on "the God of history"—as many Jews did after the Shoah. As Martin Luther once said, if we observe how God rules history and judge by any standard known to us, we must conclude "that either God is wicked or God is not" (*aut malum esse deum aut nihil esse deum*).[26]

Whatever we make of these claims, we should take time to notice that Jenson is not simply following Barth's re-working of Calvin. In a way neither Barth nor Calvin would put it, Jenson wants to insist that all things happen *within* the happening of God's will, but not quite simply *as* that happening. So long as history remains short of its end, God's will is still unfolding. Hence, his involvement in that history is not what we at first sight take it to be. He is not in fact complicit in the evil he allows, but only when everything is said and done, only when the story is fully told, will we be able to see that for the truth that it is.

God wills to be victorious for us, and for us to be "more than conquerors" in him. Therefore, he allows enemies—sin and death—as the necessary shadow-side of that victory. To say that they are shadows, that they have no being as creatures do, is not to say they are not powerful. "There is a war on between God and evil." The injustice and violence that makes our world what it is are nothing but "the stain of human angelic violence against God and against one another." War between nations is never merely "politics by other means": such violence happens as demons

26. Ibid., 77.

rise up against God. For now, God works with the grain of the universe, naturally and supernaturally, to keep these demonic forces from fulfilling their hellish purpose. So, for example, when asked why some are healed and some are not, Jenson answers:

> Because that is the will of the Lord. You know that I have Parkinson's disease. Now that is a degenerative disease. So that isn't reversible. Nevertheless, I pray to be healed, and one has to live with that. As to why there is so much suffering in the world, so much evil, that's the famous theodicy question, and in my judgment it is the only good reason not to believe in God. To say despite all the suffering in the world, God is good: that's as far as we can go.[27]

Notice, Jenson accepts that it is God's will, at least in some sense, for some to be healed and others not. And yet he also believes that we can and should pray for healing, for the miraculous, even when we have no good reason to hope for it. This is because whatever comes to us in this life, we live in hope of the eschatological accomplishment of God's will. We live awaiting the goodness of God to be accomplished; therefore, it is possible for us to pray in spite of our experiences of suffering and loss, even in spite of our commonsense awareness that our prayers are sure to go unanswered. We are confident that when God's will is finally done, our prayers—even the most outlandish and foolish ones—will be answered truly and wisely, in ways far beyond anything we could have desired or even dared to imagine.

27. Jenson, "Episode: Robert Jenson."

THE TIME WE HAVE FOR GOD

As we have seen, Jenson's theology of creation holds that creatures are made, redeemed, and glorified not only for communion with God but also by communion with him. God has opened up space within the timeliness of his own life so that we might have time for him, as well as time for one another. We are, in other words, made roomy by the roominess of God's grace, and as we become like him, we become truly ourselves.

Addressing God

All this is so, Jenson insists, because God is conversational, the lively back-and-forth that makes everything what it is. God, being God, makes creation by turning the conversation that is his life from himself to creatures. If in one way, the triune conversation makes God God—"In the beginning was the Word"—then in a different way, it makes creation creation—"God said, let there be . . . and there was."

"To be, as a creature, is to be mentioned in the triune moral conversation, as something other than those who conduct it."[28] In other words, we exist because we are invoked. And that invocation, that prayer, holds us in being and moves us toward fullness. Creation, to be itself, needs to be talked about. And the good news is that God is endlessly talkative, and his conversation is never either aimless or incoherent. God does not ramble.

The Answering Creature

Jenson makes much of the fact that in the Genesis creation narrative God creates, first, in the third person: "Let there

28. Jenson, *Systematic Theology*, 2:35.

be . . ." Then, creating human beings, God shifts to speaking in the first person plural: "Let us make . . ." In Jenson's reading, this shift from third person to first reveals, not only that God is talkative, but also that God talks about us, and then talks to us, so that we might talk about and to him in response. In a word, therefore, it is precisely our answerability to God that makes us what and who we are. According to Trinitarian dogma,

> God rightly identified . . . is to and from all eternity both subject and object of an address and its response; indeed, his being is specifiable as *conversation*. Thus the more precise form of the claim that all but God is by God's word is the claim that all but God is by and in its place in the triune conversation. Stated metaphysically, the final Christian insight into reality is that all reality is intended in a consciousness and a freedom and that this personhood is not abstract but constituted in address and answer, as are all persons.[29]

Because God speaks about us and to us, we can speak back to God and from and for God to one another and the rest of creation. But there remains this difference between God's speech and ours: what God says happens just because God says it; what we say is at best a petition for God to speak or a praise for what God has spoken. In other words, God's speech is illocutionary, ours locutionary. "When we say, 'Creatures are,' we give thanks, but when God says, 'Creatures are,' he creates."[30]

Our personal answerability to God reveals itself most impressively in prayer, in our invocation of the God who

29. Jenson, "Praying Animal," 319 (italics original).

30. Jenson, *Systematic Theology*, 2:38. See also Wright, "Creator Sings."

invokes us. In fact, for Jenson, the human being is, more than anything else, "the praying animal." Prayer, he argues, is nothing less than person-to-person communication, talking with God. "Speaking up in the divine conversation." And because God is not impersonal but a tripersonal "omnipotent conversation," we can expect answers to our prayers, whether we put them to God as petitions—"Father, I want you to do this"—or as praise—"Father, thank you for what you have done."

Freedom and Possibility

We are who and what we are because God is who and what he is. Because we can talk to God, we can talk also with one another. Because we can hear from God, we can also listen to one another. These statements are deceptively simple. And the critical truth to which they point, at least in Jenson's vision, is this: we are created to know God and ourselves the same way God knows himself and us. So, if God knows himself as a timeless essence or nature, then petitionary prayer makes little sense, if any. But if God knows himself tripersonally and dramatically, then we may be present to God with God, understood within his own self-understanding, so that he is both his own and ours— just as the risen but not yet ascended Jesus said to Mary Magdalene in the garden.

Once we have come to realize that our knowledge of God is so *personal*, we can no longer imagine that God's deity is a hindrance to his communion with us. And this realization changes everything about our understanding of prayer:

> Then our cries for help are not alien to his absolute freedom but rather constitutive of it, just as my freedom is constituted by your addresses

to me, and yours by mine. Then my telling him of my situation is not alien to his omniscience; rather this conversation between us is constitutive of his omniscience. Then his presence where two or three are gathered is not an instance of his general everywhereness but just the other way around. Then precisely humble petitionary prayer is the greatest honor we may show him.[31]

The radical dependence on God that prayer bespeaks is in fact what effects our freedom and the possibility of a true identity across time. Here, Jenson is radically Edwardsian: "I am identical with myself across time, both now and in the Kingdom, not by virtue of what is within me but by virtue of what I am within, by virtue of specific location in the unbroken life of Father, Son, and Spirit."[32] That is, we are what we are, not because have a certain substance or nature, but because we are persons ever and always called into personhood by a personal God. To be a creature at all is to be in every way related to God; to live, to move, and to have being just within the movements of God's own life.

So much modern and contemporary theology struggles to make sense of the relation of divine and human agency. As Nicholas Lash and others have shown, the Enlightenment, for all its many gifts, forced on us a way of accounting for God that imagines him as one agent among other agents, and so (at least theoretically) locatable and identifiable in the same way as everyone and everything else in existence.[33] But when God is conceived of in this way, God's freedom and our freedom are perceived to be impossibly at odds. For obvious reasons, this contradiction is most acute in modern Christologies. Christ, we moderns

31. Jenson, "What If It Were True?" 13.

32. Jenson, *On Thinking the Human*, 71.

33. See Lash, *Holiness, Speech, and Silence.*

find ourselves thinking, cannot be *both* truly, fully human *and* divine. So we tend toward kenoticizing God—as if Christ gives up his divinity so that his humanity can function freely—or toward historicizing God—as if Christ's human experience alters God for the better.[34]

In spite of the fact that he is almost always looped into the latter category by his readers, Jenson in fact refuses to take either of these paths. Drawing on Augustine, among others, he insists that "between God's will and a creature's will there is no zero-sum game, because God's deciding something in the manner of God and my deciding the same thing in the manner of a creature are not on the same plane of being."[35] What we do, we freely do—only and just because God does it. That is to say, it is precisely because God's will is absolute that our freedom is authentic. "It is precisely a divine will that cannot fail that enables creaturely freedom—indeed, nothing short of such a will could do so unlikely a thing."[36]

Jenson's Edwardsian account of human being—that our essence is nothing but God's grasp of us, God's word about us—means that human freedom is not a possession or attribute, but "something that happens to us" by the happening that is God's life. We are free because God invokes and provokes us, because we are in community with the Trinity. As Jenson frames it in his *Systematics*, "The freedom by which we as persons participate in the divine life is the very Spirit that evokes all life, all the dynamic processes of creation." We are rapt by God into a share in his freedom.[37]

34. Tanner, *Jesus, Humanity, and the Trinity*, 10.

35. Jenson, *On Thinking the Human*, 37.

36. Jenson, "Bride of Christ," 4.

37. Jenson, *On Thinking the Human*, 41.

Election: How Time Saves Us

This rapture takes place always in the now of encounter with God, as Christ makes himself present to us—above all, in the liturgical, charismatic, missional, and diaconal ministries of the church; the preaching of the evangel; and the celebration of the sacraments. Framing the issue thus makes it so that many of the familiar problems about predestination and election are rendered moot. So, if someone were to ask, "How do I know I am among the elect?" the confessor's right answer must be, "You know because I am about to absolve you, and my doing that *is* God's eternal act of decision about you." Romans 1:4 testifies to the right-now-ness and sacramentality of election: Christ's being raised from the dead does not merely confirm what was already true otherwise. It is the enactment of the truth coming to be in and for God, and precisely in that way also in and for creation.

Traditionally, emphasis falls on the need to hold together divine transcendence and immanence. For example, as Kallistos Ware puts it, there are two "poles" in our experience of God: "God is further from us, and nearer to us, than anything else."[38] Paradoxically, the nearer we come to one of these poles, the more forcefully we find ourselves drawn to the other. It is true, as Nicholas Cabasilas hymns, that God is "more affectionate than any friend, / more just than any ruler, / more loving than any father, / more a part of us than our own limbs, / more necessary to us than our own heart."[39] But it is also true that the one who approaches is truly unapproachable. He is both the light of the world and the light that we cannot draw near to—and the one because of the other.

38. Ware, *The Orthodox Way*, 12.
39. Quoted in ibid.

So far, so familiar. But Jenson unsurprisingly makes a more direct, and more radical claim. Citing John of Damascus, he insists that we are nothing less than "co-embodiments of Christ." Flesh of his flesh, bone of his bone. Construing God's relation to creation in these "hyper-Cyrillian" terms makes it abundantly clear that God's freedom is never and could never be compromised by engagement with creatures. As Stephen Wright explains, "God is transcendent precisely in his immanence. No dialectic is required . . . Every immanent encounter between God and creation is that of the Singer to the song. There is no need to protect God from the contingency of history, as the triune God transcends history, not by removal from it, but by every divine encounter with it."[40]

It is the living Christ, the transcendent and immanent one, the risen and crucified one, who is present to us in immediate encounter of mutual availability as the coherence of the Father's and the Spirit's love for us. And because he is resurrected, he may surprise us—as only the living do. The gospel's claim, "Christ is risen," means nothing less than that "we may await surprises dramatically appropriate to his life of unconditional hope" and surprises "dramatically appropriate also as the fulfillment of our life, in all its individuality, glory, and alienation."[41] Because Christ is alive, living on the far side of death, and because the Spirit comes to us from that time, that future, we can be sure that everything that the Father desires for us will be delightfully accomplished.

In this way, Jenson's doctrine of creation anticipates both his soteriology and his eschatology: if at first, before the beginning, there was only God and nothing, then at last, after the end, creation must find its fulfilment in God

40. Wright, "Creator Sings," 979.
41. Jenson, *Story and Promise*, 44.

or its dissolution in nothingness.[42] For creation to find that fulfilment in God it must be transfigured, made apt for that fulfilment. And this is precisely what God has brought about in Jesus for us.

42. Jenson, "Aspects of a Doctrine of Creation," 22.

4

SALVATION

Story & Promise

Jenson never tired of reminding his readers that the gospel is "the story about Jesus, told as a promise." And that grace is nothing but God acting savingly on us. But what does the story promise? And how does God fulfill that promise gracefully? The story promises a future in God. Or, to say the same thing another way, it promises God's future to creation as its own.[1] And God fulfills that promise by taking creaturely reality up into his life and thereby transforming it. Salvation, in other words, is participatory and theotic. As Jenson says it, "deification is our end."[2]

---

1. Jenson says his dissatisfaction with so-called dialectical theology is its refusal to accept that promise has actual content, that it can be fulfilled without being negated.

2. Jenson, "Aspects of a Doctrine of Creation," 23.

THE PROMISE OF GOD

Drawing on his Lutheran inheritance, Jenson distinguishes
two types of discourse: one, "law," which binds the future
to the past; the other, "gospel," which binds the past to the
future. Law throws us back on ourselves and on our own
understanding of the past.[3] Gospel, by contrast, throws
us onto God and neighbor, and to the Spirit's revelation
of the future. Hence, law talk has one pattern: if you do *x*,
then *y*. And gospel talk has another, rival pattern: because
God has done *x*, therefore *y*. Law, by its very structure,
imposes stipulations and conditions. But the gospel, by its
very structure, obliterates them. Because it binds the past
to the future and not the other way around, it is offered in
the present absolutely and unconditionally. It promises, *no
matter what has happened* and *no matter your present state*,
the future is now open for your good.

For Jenson, the *what* of the gospel is inseparable from
the *how* of its sharing; form and content are one and the
same. Hence, the gospel must be presented freshly each
time. As he says in *Story and Promise*—the work that marks
the beginning of his mature thought—"precisely to be itself, the gospel is never told the same way twice." Jesus is
the same yesterday, today, and forever, to be sure. But the
way we tell his story must change (without ever becoming
a different story), because the same formulas that worked
yesterday to set people free, today and tomorrow will simply bind them to the (religious) past. "'Jesus in Israel' is a
narrative . . . When it is told in any mode, and when the
real hopes and fears of those who speak and hear it are
discussed at the same time, and when the two manners of

3. Jenson, *Knowledge of Things Hoped For*, 232.

speaking mutually interpret one another, the gospel takes place."[4] Jenson provides a telltale example:

> "We are justified by faith alone," said Luther, and liberated four generations. When preachers say these words today, supposing themselves to be following Luther, they bind us to the terrible law of having to save ourselves by the quality of our sincerity, for that is what "faith" has come to mean since the eighteenth century. And who knows what "justified" might mean, without lengthy explanations?[5]

This is why the church must always give attention to theology, finding more faithful ways of speaking the gospel in particular times and places—work that is never finished, for obvious reasons. Maintaining the church's message necessitates finding new modes of speaking the gospel that are coherent both with the canonical Scriptures and the Christian dogmatic tradition, as well as effective in concrete situations for particular people, addressing their concerns and fears, their ambitions and desires. Needless to say, Jenson risks putting forward his own work as an exemplary attempt—or series of attempts—at just that kind of coherent effectiveness.

THE EROTICS OF SALVATION

God desires to save us: this is the heart, the taproot, or the leitmotif of Jenson's soteriology. As he puts it in his commentary on Song of Songs, "in the Song's allegory—and indeed in the Scriptures generally—it is not so much God who is fascinating and terrible for us, as we who are fascinating

---

4. Jenson, "Aspekte der Christologie," 115.

5. Jenson, *Story and Promise*, 11.

and terrible for God."[6] This fascination, this desire, comes at great cost: God is "overwhelmed in his fascination, even unto death on a cross." Religion—our common-sense structures of meaning and the pietistic technologies that they require—has it exactly backward: we do not desire a God who must be appeased to receive us graciously; God desires us who are too afraid or too confused or too indifferent to know how to respond rightly to the grace we have been given. Jenson admits that "all religion is doubtless in some way lovesickness for the one God," but he nevertheless maintains that it stands under the judgment of God revealed in "the baby 'mewling and puking' in his mother's lap, to quote Martin Luther, or the man on the cross, 'without form or comeliness, that we should desire him.'"[7] When the gospel comes, religion comes undone.

Freed from the fear of death that makes religion powerful, we are freed to respond to the God who loves us. Once our eyes are opened, we see that indeed the Lord is simply lovable—lovely, comely, beautiful, desirable—and that our salvation is union with him, "a union for which sexual union provides an analogy." Coming to desire God just as we are desired by him—this is the story of our salvation. Or, as Bernard of Clairvaux has it, the deepest saintliness is in loving ourselves for God's sake.

Needless to say, God's *eros* does not overwhelm God in the same way that our *eros* overwhelms us. God is driven by nothing but God. God is never controlled by anything other than his own will. But his desires *are* ecstatic in some sense: he is taken out of himself—into himself: these are the very "movements" that make the divine life lively. God desires God, and therefore in desiring us, God is simply being

6. Jenson, *Song of Songs*, 67.
7. Ibid.

true to himself. And by being true to himself, God delivers us from our fear, our confusion, our indifference.

Paul claims he received his call "in hope of eternal life, which God, who cannot lie, promised before times eternal, but in his own time manifested his word in the message of the gospel." (Titus 1:2–3). Notice that "before" creation—in "times eternal"—God *promises* the hope of eternal life. To whom could God make such a promise? Only to himself, of course. Therefore, Jenson concludes, the one who justifies the ungodly must be triune. And justification itself must be a "triune event," as the righteous Father speaks the word of forgiveness and reconciliation, the Son, Jesus, entails the event of that reconciliation in his life, death, and resurrection, and the Spirit brings about the fulfillment of all righteousness—both for God and for us.[8]

"While We Were Yet Sinners"

Scripture insists that God loves us precisely as sinners, as creatures made ugly by our own wrongdoing. Thinking in these terms commits Jenson to a version of supralapsarianism: the incarnation, as he understands it, is "neither an emergency measure nor construable apart from sin . . . the gospel of forgiveness is not an afterthought."[9] But what sense does it make to say that God purposes sin and yet is not the cause of evil and is not himself wicked? Jenson follows Barth: God purposes sin only as negation, as that which is overcome by Christ's death and life. Evil is nothing—a nothing that goodness makes possible precisely by destroying it.

Does this not make God a moral monster? Or, at least, does it not show he is irreconcilably self-conflicted?

8. Jenson, "Justification as Triune Event," 426.

9. Jenson, *Systematic Theology*, 1:73.

No, Jenson says, because God's character as triune spirit of love is made known in devotion to that which is radically other than himself. In this sense, the sinner loved by a holy God is a nearer analog to the triune life than the saint who shares in God's holiness. But of course in another sense, the saint who shares in God's divine-human holiness is no longer a mere analog to the triune life: she embodies it and is embodied in it. Hence, when all is said and done, only those who are aware of their state as simultaneously saint and sinner can fully articulate to the rest of creation what it is for God to be God.

"He Justifies the Ungodly"

We are justified, Jenson says, by "God's sheer declaration." But what, exactly, is declared? Not just that we are forgiven. What is declared is the final judgment about us: "the word of the gospel . . . is the eschatological judgment let out ahead of time."[10] God says we are now what in truth we shall only be then. We are already what we are not yet.

The divine declaration is not merely forensic or juridical. Jenson holds that there is no "legal fiction" involved, because God cannot lie, since what the Father speaks, happens, through the Spirit in the life of the Son.[11] Following a "Finnish" reading of Luther, Jenson argues that the declaration of justification effects the union of the hearer's heart with the gospel-word, and precisely in that way the union of the believer with Christ, "who is speaker and content of that word."[12] As Mannerma says, "in the ontological mutuality of word and faith, Christ and the believing soul make but one entity, so that when God—the Father!—attributes

10. Jenson, "Theosis," 112.

11. Jenson, *Song of Songs*, 45.

12. Jenson, "Theosis," 112.

Christ's divine righteousness to the believer, he is only registering the truth."[13]

"We Die With Him"

We are not yet done with paradoxes. God is death's opponent.[14] And yet he defeats death—and the fear of death—for us by dying, and by incorporating us into that death.

> Cross and resurrection are the fact, and that puts love and death into a new relation. Does the gift of love lead to the death of the lover? Yes, it led Christ to death for us. Does the desire of love lead to death of the beloved? Yes, Christ's desire for us took and takes us with him into death: "we have been buried with him by baptism into death" (Rom. 6.4).[15]

But because Christ has passed through death, and now lives and loves with death behind him, we can live boldly: "We can take the risk of giving ourselves to the beloved and of loving the beloved's own self," because we know that even if this leads to death for us—and it inevitably must—it is merely "death unto new life." A share in Christ's already-inaugurated resurrection awaits; therefore, we have nothing to fear. If it is true that "our only hope is God's personal stake in the good he wills for us,"[16] then we have all hope, because God has taken that personal stake into death—and beyond.

It is easy to get lost in this tangle. But if it seems that Jenson has drifted free of Scripture into sheer speculation, consider what Paul says in Romans (11:29–32):

13 Quoted in Jenson, "Justification as a Triune Event," 425.

14. Jenson, *Systematic Theology*, 1:66.

15. Jenson, *Song of Songs*, 95.

16. Jenson, *Ezekiel*, 63.

> For the gifts and the calling of God are without repentance. For as in time past you were disobedient, but now have received mercy through their disobedience, even so have they also now been disobedient, that by the mercy shown to you they also may now receive mercy. For God has shut up all in disobedience, that he might have mercy on all.

Clearly, Paul is convinced that God is involved in the hurly-burly of history, acting in ways none of us can trace, using the disobedience of the many for the good of the few, and the obedience of the few for the salvation of the many. And how does God accomplish this mystery? By the wisdom revealed in the cross, the wisdom of divine foolishness.

THE SATISFACTION OF GOD

Salvation, for Jenson, is theosis. But we cannot understand what it means for us to be delivered from sin and death into the life of God unless and until we have some sense of what the life of God is and how it happens. For example, if we do not know what it is for God to be righteous, how can we understand what it means for God to make us righteous? Whatever we do, we must not trust our commonsense understanding of righteousness. We must, instead, look to the story of Jesus, the story told by the canonical Scriptures, and ask what that tells us about God. And what the story tells us, at least as Jenson reads it, is that *righteousness* names actual faithfulness in and to community. "As this occurs in God, the Trinitarian tradition calls it *perichoresis*."[17] As this occurs outwith God, we call it salvation. Just as God creates a history to share with us, so God delivers us from the mere contingencies of history by sharing his life with us. What

17. Jenson, "Justification as Triune Event," 426.

satisfies God is God; and that is precisely what satisfies us, as well. God being true to himself and being true to us are the same event.

Here, Jenson sides with (his reading of) the Cappadocians over against (his reading of) Saint Augustine and the majority view of the Western theological tradition:

> Augustine's God has no room in himself for us; he cannot bless us with himself. He can only bless us in our externality to him, with "created" gifts, with restorations and improvements of our own human nature. If God is as Western theology normally thinks him, then to "become Gods" could indeed only mean an alteration of natures . . . an intrusion on God's uniqueness.[18]

But if the Cappadocians (and a minority of Western theologians, including Jenson's beloved Jonathan Edwards) were right, then we do not share the *nature* of God, but the tripersonal, dramatic *life* of God. Jenson summarizes it so: "we can become God because the true God, the *triune* God whose unity is founded by his mutual plurality, has room in himself for others."[19] As he puts it in his *Systematics*, God is roomy, and can include us in his life without violating either his nature or ours, his creatorliness or our creatureliness. In the language of Scripture, God is our life, so that we are truly hidden in Christ's experience within the happening of the divine being. "The difference of Creator and creature is eternal, but precisely because God is the infinite Creator, there can be no limit to the modes and degrees of creatures' promised participation in his life."[20]

And that brings us to the doctrine of the church.

18. Jenson, "Theosis," 110.

19. Ibid., 109–10.

20. Jenson, "Church as *Communio.*"

5

CHURCH

Anticipation & Availability

The church, as Jenson regards it, is an anticipation of the kingdom, a kind of prefiguration of the age to come, an embodiment now of the promise that is not yet realized for all creation. As such, the church is the availability of Christ to the world, and the church's ministries mark the nexus of time and eternity, earth and heaven, past and future where God is personally encountered by those he graciously draws to himself in faith. All creatures are moved by God to their end, to be sure. But the church is doubly moved, because as the body of Christ it is a creature that through its ministries mediates the movement of the other creatures toward God. That is to say, the church shares in Christ's mission, and so exists for the sake of bringing the world to awareness of the hope that has been given it in his resurrection. The church is nothing but this mission, as it is nothing but the ministry of Christ taking a particular communal shape.

THE EXISTENCE OF THE CHURCH

In her unique availability as mediating community, the church exists in three modes: as the people of God, the body of Christ, and the temple of the Spirit. These three modalities coinhere in one reality. As Jenson reads them, the figures—people, body, temple—perfectly explicate one another.[1] All three are upheld in existence by anticipation of creation's deifying end in God:

> God's one People will not gather until the last day; therefore the church can now be the People of God only in anticipation of that gathering, as the community that lives by what God will eschatologically make of it. The church is the Body of that Christ whose bodily departure to God's right hand his disciples once witnessed, and whose return of like fashion we must still await. The church is the Temple of that Spirit whose very reality among us is "down-payment," "*arrabon*."[2]

First, the church is the temple of the Spirit in the sense that the church is a place the Spirit makes of God's people as foretaste or foreglimpse of the eschatological kingdom. John of Damascus says that the Spirit rests on the body of the Son, the *totus Christus*. Second, the church is the people of God in the sense that she has to be one as God is one and holy as God is holy in order to be truly apostolic and catholic.[3] That is, if the church hopes to "run with God," to live with the one whom the prophets and apostles lovingly feared, then the church has to be radically different from

1. Jenson, *Systematic Theology*, 2:190.

2. Jenson, "Church as *Communio*," 2.

3. This aligns the church with Israel in nonsupersessionist way. The church is not the people of God instead of or in competition with Israel, but alongside Israel.

everything else in creation.[4] Finally, the church is the body of Christ in that she is how the risen and ascended Jesus is yet available to be seen and heard as well as to be touched and spoken to by those whom he loves.

Notice how all of this assumes that the church with her Lord is simply the *totus Christus*. The church, in short, is "the fullness of him who fills all things with himself," the authority to which God subjects all things (Eph 1:22–23). In Jenson's own words, the church is Christ "as Christ is in the world and therefore available in the world." That means, among other things, that if the world wants to rid itself of Christ and the God he reveals, then it has to persecute the church because that is where Christ can be touched. Conversely, if the world wants to learn from Christ and to worship the God he reveals, "all it has to do is listen to the church, because again that is the thing as which he is to be found."[5] What happens to Christ happens to his body. What happens to his body happens to him.

Of course, not all of the churches—and none of them all of the time—are everything the church is revealed in Scripture and declared at every Eucharist-event to be. To be faithful, we must be spurred on, wooed toward the fullness of Christ's stature as the perfection of all things. "We rely on the church as on the presence of God, [but] we do so just in that the church within herself directs us to a presence of God that is not identical with herself."[6] And far too often, she fails even to do this.

How can Jenson say both that the church is Christ's body, one Spirit with him as surely as Eve was one flesh with Adam, and that the church is often deeply unfaithful? To ask the same question another way, if it is true, as Jenson

4. Jenson, *Theology in Outline*, 94.

5. Ibid., 97.

6. Jenson, *Systematic Theology*, 2:167.

often insists, that the mystery of the church is that God's Spirit is her spirit, then how can it be that the churches fail? And what can Christ do about the failures of his own body? Jenson typically addresses this problem on two fronts at once: first, he talks about Christ's correction of the church as a kind of "self-discipline," and he talks about the church as also the *bride* of Christ, who is wooed into faithful oneness with her groom:

> The identity of Christ embodied for the church with Christ embodied as the church is constituted in that the one embodiment anticipates itself in the other. Thus Paul's bridal metaphor is eschatological: what is now is the engagement and Paul's care for its success, the wedding itself is the consummation to come. In this, he joins the Revelation, where the Old Testament's discourse of Israel as the Lord's bride massively resurfaces, but now in unambiguously eschatological context: the final event of the Revelation's drama is "the marriage of the Lamb," for which "his Bride has made herself ready" (Rev. 19:7).[7]

THE MINISTRIES OF THE CHURCH

The church is a community with a message. In other words, it exists just to get the gospel said in the world for God's and the world's sake. The church delivers that message both to God and to the world and gets it said in words visible and audible—that is, in sacraments and in preaching, and in the culture that makes the celebration of the sacraments and preaching intelligible.

For Jenson, as for Luther, these public kerygmatic ministries of the church are the heart of the ascended

7. Jenson, "Bride of Christ," 4.

Christ's ongoing work in the world. "The consecrated bread and cup on the altar, the mouth of the preacher and the open page of the Scripture, the basin or torrent of water—and however many other sacramental *signa* there may be . . . mark the earthly places to which we may look to be looking to heaven, to the whence of God's coming; they are the created markers setting the boundary within creation which God rends to come to us."[8] And they must get said as *promise* and not as *law*. Otherwise, they are not truly what they must be.

Sacraments, as Jenson describes them, are signs that get done what they signify. And what they signify is an anticipated reality—the reality of the kingdom. They are signs of this age that indicate and just so mediate a reality of the age to come. "A Christian sacrament brings into the present some aspect of the future promised by the gospel."[9] As he articulates it in his commentary on the *Song*, "Where the Lord comes, in the reading of Torah or the celebration of Eucharist or in any of a hundred events of his 'real presence' among his people, something of the final and first-intended fulfillment opens to our experience; we are in 'the gate of heaven,' as Martin Luther described the church."[10]

Baptism is the sacrament that creates the church, as birth is the event that determines the human community. According to the New Testament, baptism "saves" (1 Pet 1:3–21). And it is in baptism that believers are joined in the fellowship of Christ's disciples and just so into God's own life (Matt 28:19). This means that the fullness of the

8. Jenson, "On the Ascension," 335.

9. Jenson, *Ezekiel*, 57. Against the pressure of most Protestantism, especially in the United States, Jenson argues that the Christian faith is inherently, necessarily sacramental. A version of the faith that denies sacramentality is necessarily deviant.

10. Jenson, *Song of Songs*, 35.

Christian life is anticipated in the event of baptism: for example, the church is a community of those who have been justified and sanctified; therefore, baptism's work is described in the Scriptures as justifying and sanctifying (1 Cor 1:26–31; 6:8–11); the church is a community of priests and prophets; therefore, baptism is described as "the anointing by which priests and prophets are made" (Heb 10:22; 1 John 2:18–27); the church is persecuted but victorious; therefore, baptism is described as "incorporation into the risen Christ's own body and into dying and rising with and in him" (Rom 6:1–11). All this means believers are always trying to "catch up" to their baptism, hoping to realize in their lives the fullness of the reality brought to bear on them in the waters of blessing.

Eucharist is the sacrament of Christ's present embodiment for his people, the means by which he constitutes them as his body for the sake of the world. If the world wants to find Christ, then it must look to the church. If the church wants to find Christ, it must look to the Eucharist: "the place where he can be found, where he can be located, is the bread and cup on the table or on the altar."[11] Not as a second body alongside the church, but as that same body in a different mode of availability.

Again, the Eucharist is a meal that makes a promise: "The meal-fellowship of the Supper is the acted-out promise of the last fellowship. To be brought into the fellowship of this Supper is to anticipate belonging to the fellowship of the kingdom."[12] If we eat the meal in any other spirit, coming to the Table out of mere ritualism or self-seeking, we consume judgment on ourselves. For example, if the cup is not shared spiritedly, joyfully, then everything is lost. And

11. Jenson, *Theology in Outline*, 85.

12. Jenson, *Visible Words*, 79.

the same is true if we refuse to live together the covenant the thanksgiving-cup makes for us.[13]

In the Eucharist, Christ is present in a way that joins him to his own people so that he and his body are at-one-ed, and so that each member is thereby at-one-ed with the other members. Just as the bread is bread and yet body because it has become through the Spirit a sign of eschatological reality, and just as the wine is wine and yet blood because it has been transformed by its very reality as Spirit-baptized sign, so the church is the church and yet Christ's body, and Christ is God and yet creature. In short, the Eucharist is the sign that makes the church the church, just as the church is the sign that makes the world the world.

Ordination is the sacrament that centers the Christian community in its continuity with the apostles and its fidelity to the message entrusted to its care. But even if there should be an order of ministry—bishops, in succession, flanked by deacons and presbyters—only God is sovereign, and all believers are invited into "common parliament with him, that is, to common prayer."[14] Just at this point, the church's difference from all worldly order and disorder comes to the fore:

> In the church, the inner flaw of all this world's polities, our inevitable lust to dominate, is broken, because the One from whom we would here seek to wrest freedom cannot be dominated. In the church, all the baptized are invited to the table, where the host so gives himself to them that they have nothing more to wrest from him or from one another."[15]

13. Ibid., 83.
14 Jenson, *On Thinking the Human*, 44.
15. Ibid.

Preaching, as Jenson regards it, is a word-event that makes the gospel happen for speaker and hearers alike. As such, it is the proof of any theology. In his own preaching, Jenson models what he takes to be the criterion for faithful preaching: wrestling with the plain christological sense of whatever texts the lectionary assigns in the effort to awaken in hearers the kind of faith that radically alters their relation to their own past, opening them to possibilities before unimaginable of loving others. Preaching, in other words, must be the happening of the good news. For a sermon to be truly a Word of God, hearers must not merely think or feel differently—they must be moved in fact by the Spirit toward Christ as their Lord and toward his Father.

The church, as Jenson understands it, is something like a culture that stands in contrast with all other cultures, existing over against all worldly orders and disorders. In the language of Ephesians and Colossians, the church is a witness against the powers of this age because it is subject only to Christ, who has dethroned the powers in his death and resurrection, and who has been established by the Spirit as Lord of all. But what kind of culture is the church? Jenson notes that ethnography uses *culture* to name all the practices and customs that hold a community together across time and space. The church has such practices and customs—including, for example, preaching, Eucharist, baptism, intercessory prayer, ordination—although of course they are adapted to the needs of particular communities in particular contexts.[16] Above all, the church is a culture of *revolution*, participating in whatever penultimate revolutions prove necessary, in full knowledge that Jesus is the only revolutionary who can guarantee a revolution that does not in the end defeat itself.

16. For an example of how Jenson expects this adaptation to play out in a non-Western society, see Jenson, "Risen Prophet."

Only the one could create a real revolution who would have lived in freedom to the end of the established structures—without abandoning the historical, human reality mediated in these structures. That is to say, only the one could make a revolution who would have freely given up his life and would have died of his complete acceptance of the hating, alienated, and counter-revolutionary fellow human beings. There will be revolution when it is made by a loving one who died for his love. We who say that Jesus is risen, say that there is such a man, and expect *the* revolution. For this very reason, we are free to use revolutionary pathos in penultimate "revolutions" without disappointment.[17]

In other words, the church is revolutionary most of all in its participation in worldly revolutions, because it alone never forgets that Christ alone can overturn all evil for the good of all. And it is that hope that constitutes the meaning of the longed-for kingdom of God.

17. Jenson, ""Aspekte der Christologie," 115.

6

KINGDOM

The End as Music

From the beginning of his career, from long before he knew the term *theology of hope* or the movement it names, Jenson was a theologian of hope. The entire force of his theology arises from the expectation that God has made time for us, and that the gospel promises God's future as the fulfillment of our history. The end of our history must be truly an ending—like the ending of a good story. And the end of our history must be somehow also a beginning (although, of course, of a radically different kind from what we have come to know as beginnings). All this can take place only because God himself is inherently dramatic, and "he shares our history in time as his history," so directing the drama as beginning, goal, and guide.[1]

1. Jenson, *Ezekiel*, 72.

THE COMING OF THE END

But how does that end come? And what happens in its coming? It comes as manifestation, judgment, reconciliation, fulfillment, and bliss: all of these at once, and each because of the others. And this manifold end can come about only by a divine work that effects creation's translation into God's own life.

Manifestation

Scripture promises that the Father's "manifestation of our Lord Jesus Christ" will be brought about "at the right time" (1 Tim 6:14). But Jenson's account of God's relation to time makes it clear that Christ's "manifestation" is not an event *within* time, or even *after* time, but an event that happens *to* time. Instead of the *terminus* of God's grace, Christ's "manifestation" is its *telos*.

Jesus's coming in glory necessarily alters the very structures of reality. The apocalyptic moment at time's end is no less decisive than the primordial moment at time's beginning. And like that beginning, that end is not one moment among other moments but the final, consummating moment that happens to all moments. For Jenson, the manifestation or appearing of Christ is not *a* moment after all other moments, but *the* moment in which all moments, all events, are drawn into the light of the divine glory where they are truly what they are.

The Gospels show that even before his glorification, Jesus's incarnate presence affected everyone and everything around him. How much more so in the End, when he is presenced in glory? How could his glorious appearing, his all-revealing manifestation, not alter time itself in such a way that all times—and everything that happened in them—are opened to him? When the firstborn of all creation, the one in whom all things hold together, makes himself known in *this* manner, everything hidden must be revealed, everything lost must be found, everything broken must be healed, everything wrong must be righted.

Judgment

"I will be cured without being eradicated."[2] That is the promise of the Last Judgment. And only such a judgment, enacted by the triune God, could both bring our history to fulfillment and open up a new history for us. The judgment that Christ's appearing effects is not merely a reckoning for wrongs done, or merely a delivery of final verdicts on the state of our character, not a simple weighing of balances or dispensing of grades. Instead, it is a *generative* event, the "moment" in which God acts unrestrictedly and fully on creation. In this way, God consummates what he has already initiated in Israel and the church.

Reconciliation

Jesus is the truth; therefore, for him to be present to all creation in the fullness of his glory means that justice—that which is most fitting, most true given the goodness and beauty of God—is both indisputably clear and irreversibly accomplished. Delivering judgment, Christ reorders creation rightly. In fact, this "setting right," Jenson insists, is "the *content* of the eternal event of bliss."[3] We tend to imagine the ending judgment as effecting *separations*. But what if we were to think of it as an alpha point of "the eternal expansion of one great *reconciling*"?[4]

2. Jenson, *On Thinking the Human*, 72.
3. Jenson, "The Great Transformation," 39.
4. Ibid. (italics original).

Jenson is abundantly clear: such reconciling will and could come about only as the perfect realization of God's holiness. God's justice must be done; therefore, no sin or injustice—not even an "idle word"!—can be ignored or forgotten. All sinners must give account for their sins. All sinned-against must receive the justice they deserve. If in Christ we know that God is light and that in him there's no darkness at all, if eternal life is nothing less than being taken up into God, if in the end all the works of the enemy must be destroyed, then we must at last become righteous just as he is righteous—"very light of very light." Sanctification is the condition of our existence.

But we must bear in mind it is *God's* justice that must be done, not our own. And the character of God's justice has already been made plain in the face of Jesus Christ. To finally, truly see *that* face—how could it not bring the beauty of holiness to bear upon us in ways that determine our being, once and always, now and forever?

Fulfillment

Jenson, following Jonathan Edwards, insists that the eschaton does not merely happen to us, but also comes from us. Judged, we are also judges. The end witnesses the realization of the promise that "God has taken his place in the divine council; in the midst of the gods he holds judgment" (Ps 82:1). With God, we judge—and are judged by—one another, the world, and the angels. Jenson appeals to Edwards, who makes the point forcefully: Christ's promises to the apostles are not fulfilled until we, like all who follow Christ, share in his judgment in the glorious end of all things (see Matt 19:28; Luke 22:30).

Bliss

In the end, the saints find their bliss in seeing God and all things in God. In Jenson's words,

> Christ will know himself as his people with no more reservation; he will be head of a body that he does not need to discipline. Thus he will eternally adore God *as* the one single and exclusive person of the *totus Christus,* as those whom the Father ordained for him and whom the Spirit has brought to him.[5]

On this point, as so often on other points, Jenson is building on Jonathan Edwards's speculations. Edwards, drawing on claims in Matt 11:27 and John 6:46, insists that only the Son knows God immediately, while all other creatures know God via means, that is, by "manifestations or signs." Jesus, in Edwards's phrase, is "the grand medium" in which all other means have their being, and by which they are judged. In the eschaton, then, Edwards believes that the saints will see God *mediately* in seeing Christ—and through all of the other creaturely means of grace that the Son draws into his service. Above all, these other means are the creatures, angelic and human, who are "endowed with holiness" so that they share Christ's character, his image. The saints "converse with God" in the world to come by "conversing with Christ, who speaketh the words of God."[6]

In Jenson's paraphrase of Aquinas, "deification and the beatific vision coincide."[7] In the language of Scripture's promise, "we shall be like him" because "we shall see him as he is" (1 John 3:2). And we shall know as we are known (1 Cor 13:12). Our hearts, renewed by the Spirit, long for

5. Jenson, *Systematic Theology,* 2:339 (italics original).

6. Edwards, *Miscellanies 777.*

7. Jenson, *Systematic Theology,* 2:344.

that more than for anything: "I shall be satisfied, seeing your likeness" (Ps 17:15). Even now, we anticipate that vision every time we gather around the Table to hear the Scriptures read and the gospel preached, and to share in the eucharistic meal. As Jenson puts it, "we will know ourselves [then] as Christ's body as directly as we now know the signs of bread and cup."[8] Every Eucharist, then, is a foretaste of our eschatological existence.

THE NATURE OF ESCHATOLOGICAL EXISTENCE

Jenson is clear that our share in Christ's resurrection at his coming effects the creation of "a new material world." "The achievement of God's reign" will mean an end of one world and the beginning of another.[9] But what will our life be like in this new order of existence? As Jenson envisions it, it will be an existence of new bodies and new times, new ministry and new politics, new pleasures and endless surprises.

New Bodies, New Times

Whenever we pray the creed, we confess our desire for the resurrection of the body and the life everlasting for which resurrected bodies are made. But what kind of embodiment is promised to us in that everlastingly resurrected life? Jenson is blunt: "a body in the new creation must indeed be a something, and a material something." What kind of materiality? Whatever materiality is fitted to the knowing God as he knows himself. Jenson references the vision of Gottfried Thomasius, a nineteenth-century Lutheran theologian: "the new spiritual body will be much more the

8. Jenson, "Eschatology," 416.
9. Jenson, *Systematic Theology*, 2:348.

transparent expression of the sanctified person, the bright mirror of his inner purity and moral beauty."[10]

New embodiment requires a new temporality. Saint Augustine discerned that we, in this "physical" body, necessarily experience time only in losing it. Time exists, he says in book 11 of his *Confessions*, only in that it passes into the past, dying to us. The jagged edges of this truth gash us whenever we realize what time's passing means for our relationship with those we love most deeply. But then, our bodies, like the time/space they inhabit, shall be of such a nature that *nothing* is lost. And all that had been lost shall be restored. As Moltmann explains, "In the 'restoration of all things,' all times will return and—transformed and transfigured—will be taken up into the aeon of the new creation."[11] To move to poetics, which Jenson insists we must do, we can say that God will turn the water of history into the wine of eternity; the "loaves and fishes" of our worldly experience will be taken up and multiplied infinitely in the banquet that is our knowing as we are known. "Only *this* can be called 'the fulness of the times.'"[12] Or, as Jenson himself puts it, "Eternal life is rather the infinite appropriation and interpretation of accomplished lives within the discourse of the triune life."[13]

New Ministry, New Politics

Like N. T. Wright, Jürgen Moltmann, and others, Jenson holds that the gospel promises in the end the *marriage* of heaven and earth, a (re)new(ed) cosmos in which God's will is finally, perfectly accomplished "on earth as it is in

10. Quoted in ibid., 2:356.

11. Moltmann, *Coming of God*, 294–95.

12. Ibid.

13. Jenson, "Eschatology," 415.

heaven."[14] But Jenson is perhaps clearest in his insistence that our hope, then, is in the absolute establishment of God's polity, the "New Jerusalem," as the political and cultural center of the 'new heavens and new earth, where righteousness dwells." Jenson poses the shift in Augustinian terms:

> "Two loves make the two polities, love of self the earthly polity . . . , love of God the heavenly." The distinction is eschatological. Every created self will pass away; indeed, love of self is the very principle of historical decay: "He that seeks his life will lose it." Love of God will not pass away, for he is what all things pass on to. Thus the gates of hell will sooner or later prevail against every polity of this age. They will not prevail against the church, which will be fulfilled precisely by the judgment that burns away its accommodations to this age.[15]

New Pleasures, New Surprises

We have the promise of new bodies and new times. But what will we *do* with those bodies in those times? Jenson, following Edwards, imagines that the "saints' glorified bodies shall be attuned to every physical pleasure, in a way that shall not inhibit but only add to their spiritual pleasure."[16] In Edwards's own words, "Every perceptive faculty shall be an inlet of delight."[17] Can we speak, then, of an eternally

14. See, for example, Wright, *Paul and the Faithfulness of God*, 1043–1265; Moltmann, *The Coming of God*; and Pannenberg, *Systematic Theology*, vol. 3.

15. Jenson, "Eschatology," 413.

16. Edwards, "Miscellanies" no. 233, in *Works*, 13:350–51.

17. Quoted in Caldwell, "Brief History of Heaven," 67.

sanctified sensuality? With Edwards, Jenson gives a hearty yes!

> After all, will there be no jewelers or goldsmiths in the Kingdom? And will the achievement of their lives provide no matter for eternal interpretation by Jesus' love? The feast of "rich food ... of well-aged wines strained clear," will it have no taste? Will there no be cooks or vintners in the Kingdom? Or even connoisseurs?[18]

If Israel's and the church's experiences with God prove anything, it is that God, while faithful, is never predictable. God is, perhaps above all, *surprising*. Hence, after all has been said and done, after all our efforts to find the least inadequate ways to give voice to reasons for the hope that makes our lives livable, we have to say simply this: whatever happens in the End will be better, more just, and more beautiful than we can now imagine. "No eye has seen, nor ear heard, nor the human heart conceived, what God has prepared for those who love him" (1 Cor 2:8).

The end is music, Jenson says. God is a fugue, and so creation's end must be translation into that movement. Creation happens as "creatures are summoned into being as this song opens up to allow the participation of singers other than the triune persons."[19] Creation's consummation happens as these same creatures come to sing their song in ever more glorious, ever more beautiful harmony with God's own singing.

I once heard an architect say that music, unlike paintings or sculpture, cannot be turned away from, because it surrounds you, envelops you. That, it seems to me, is what Jenson means for us to hear: in the end, God will truly,

18. Jenson, *Systematic Theology*, 2:352.

19. Wright, "Creator Sings," 977.

fully surround us, as a space that has no exterior. And in enveloping us as beginning, guide, and end, God will fulfill us just as he himself is all in all. The end is music—a music that does not end, and so is always our beginning. "The harmony in God that is his beauty and the beauty of all things is a harmony of the shocks and revelations that make the history told in Scripture."[20] And so in the world without end, we shall go on experiencing these shocks and revelations in an always ascending cascade of delights.

20. Jenson, "Deus Est Ipsa Pulchritudo," 214.

Bibliography

Augustine, Daniela. "Creation as Perichoretic Trinitarian Conversation." In *The Promise of Robert Jenson's Theology: Constructive Engagements,* edited by Stephen J. Wright and Chris E. W. Green, 99–113. Minneapolis: Fortress, 2017.

Behr, John. *Irenaeus of Lyons: Identifying Christianity.* Christian Theology in Context. Oxford: Oxford University Press, 2013.

———. *The Mystery of Christ: Life in Death.* Crestwood, NY: St. Vladimir's Seminary Press, 2006.

Caldwell, Robert W., III. "A Brief History of Heaven in the Writings of Jonathan Edwards." *Calvin Theological Journal* 46/1 (2011) 48–71.

Coakley, Sarah. *God, Sexuality, and the Self: An Essay 'on the Trinity'.* Cambridge: Cambridge University Press, 2013.

Crisp, Oliver D. "Robert Jenson on the Pre-Existence of Christ." *Modern Theology* 23/1 (2007) 27–45.

Culler, Jonathan. *Literary Theory: A Very Short Introduction.* Very Short Introductions. Oxford: Oxford University Press, 1997.

Edwards, Jonathan. *The Works of Jonathan Edwards.* 26 vols. New Haven: Yale University Press, 1966–2008.

Hunsinger, George. "Robert Jenson's Systematic Theology: A Review Essay." *Scottish Journal of Theology* 55/2 (2002) 161–200.

Jenson, Robert W. "About Dialog, and the Church, and Some Bits of the Theological Biography of Robert W. Jenson." *Dialog* 11/1 (1969) 272–78.

———. *Alpha and Omega: A Study in the Theology of Karl Barth.* New York: Nelson, 1963.

———. *America's Theologian: A Recommendation of Jonathan Edwards.* New York: Oxford University Press, 1988.

———. "Aspects of a Doctrine of Creation." In *The Doctrine of Creation: Essays in Dogmatics, History, and Philosophy,* edited by Colin Gunton, 17–28. London: T. & T. Clark, 1997.

Bibliography

———. "Aspekte der Christologie in einer pluralistischen Gesellschaft." In *Christsein in einer pluralistischen Gesellschaft*, edited by Hans Schulze and Hans Schwartz, 113–17. Hamburg: Wittig, 1971.

———. "The Bride of Christ." In *Critical Issues in Ecclesiology: Essays in Honor of Carl E. Braaten*, edited by Alberto L. Garcia and Susan K. Wood, 1–5. Grand Rapids: Eerdmans, 2011.

———. *Canon and Creed*. Interpretation: Resources for the Use of Scripture in the Church. Louisville: Westminster John Knox, 2010.

———. "The Church as *Communio*." In *The Catholicity of the Reformation*, edited by Carl E. Braaten and Robert W. Jenson, 1–12. Grand Rapids: Eerdmans, 1996.

———. "Christ as Culture 2: Christ as Art." *International Journal of Systematic Theology* 6/1 (2004) 69–76.

———. "The Church as Communion: A Catholic-Lutheran Dialog-Consensus-Statement Dreamed in the Night." *Pro Ecclesia* 4 (1995) 68–78.

———. "Conceptus . . . de Spiritu Sancto." *Pro Ecclesia* 15 (2006) 100–107.

———. "Creator and Creature." *International Journal of Theology* 4/2 (2002) 216–21.

———. "Creation as a Triune Act." *Word and World* 2/1 (1982) 34–42.

———. "D. Stephen Long's *Saving Karl Barth: An Agent's Perspective*." *Pro Ecclesia* 24/2 (2015) 131–33.

———. "Deus Est Ipsa Pulchritudo." In *Theology as Revisionary Metaphysics: Essays on God and Creation*, edited by Stephen John Wright, 204–15. Eugene, OR: Cascade Books, 2014.

———. "Episode: Robert Jenson—Don't Thank Me, Thank the Holy Spirit." Interview by Jason Michelli, Kenneth Tanner, and Chris E. W. Green, *Crackers and Grape Juice* (podcast) dropped on May 4, 2017. See *Tamed Cynic* (blog) http://tamedcynic.org/episode-robert-jenson-dont-thank-me-thank-the-holy-spirit/.

———. "Eschatological Politics and Political Eschatology." In *The Futurist Option,* edited by Carl E. Braaten and Robert W. Jenson, 93–106. New York: Newman, 1970.

———. "Eschatology." In *The Blackwell Companion to Political Theology*, edited by Peter Scott and William T. Cavanaugh, 407–20. Blackwell Companions to Religion. Malden, MA: Blackwell, 2004.

————. "Evil as Person" (1989). In *Theology as Revisionary Meta-physics: Essays on God and Creation*, edited by Steven J. Wright, 136–45. Eugene, OR: Cascade Books, 2014.

————. *Ezekiel*. Brazos Theological Commentary on the Bible. Grand Rapids: Brazos, 2009.

————. "The Father, He . . ." In *Speaking of the Christian God: The Holy Trinity and the Challenge of Feminism*, edited by Alvin F. Kimel Jr., 95–109. Grand Rapids: Eerdmans, 1992.

————. *God after God: The God of the Past and the God of the Future Seen in the Work of Karl Barth*. Indianapolis: Bobbs-Merrill, 1969.

————. "The Great Transformation." In *The Last Things: Biblical and Theological Perspectives on Eschatology*, edited by Carl E. Braaten and Robert W. Jenson, 33–42. Grand Rapids: Eerdmans, 2002.

————. "The Hidden and Triune God." *International Journal of Systematic Theology* 2/1 (2000) 5–12.

————. "Ipse Pater Non Est Impassibilis." In *Divine Impassibility and the Mystery of Human Suffering*, edited by James F. Keating and Thomas Joseph White, 117–26. Grand Rapids: Eerdmans, 2009.

————. "Justification as a Triune Event." *Modern Theology* 11/4 (1995) 421–27.

————. *The Knowledge of Things Hoped For: The Sense of Theological Discourse*. New York: Oxford University Press, 1969.

————. *A Large Catechism*. Delhi, NY: American Lutheran Publicity Bureau, 1999.

————. "Liberating Truth and Liberal Education." *Lutheran Quarterly* 13/3 (1961) 211–17.

———— "On the Ascension." In *Loving God with Our Minds: The Pastor as Theologian*, edited by Michael Welker and Cynthia A. Jarvis, 331–40. Grand Rapids: Eerdmans, 2004.

————. *On the Inspiration of Scripture*. Delhi, NY: ALPB Books, 2012.

————. *On Thinking the Human: Resolutions of Difficult Notions*. Grand Rapids: Eerdmans, 2003.

————. "On Truth and God: 1." *Pro Ecclesia* 20/2 (2011) 34–38.

————. "On Truth and God: 2." *Pro Ecclesia* 21/1 (2012) 51–55.

————. "Once More the *Logos Asarkos*." *International Journal of Systematic Theology* 13/2 (2011) 130–33.

————. "The Praying Animal." *Zygon* 18/3 (1983) 311–25.

————. *A Religion against Itself*. Richmond: John Knox, 1967.

————. "Reversals: How My Mind Has Changed." *Christian Century* 127/8 (April, 2010) 30–33.

Bibliography

———. "The Risen Prophet." In *God and Jesus: Theological Reflections for Christian-Muslim Dialog*, by the American Lutheran Church Division for World Mission and Interchurch Cooperation, 57–67. Minneapolis: American Lutheran Church, 1986.

———. "A Second Thought about Inspiration." *Pro Ecclesia* 13/4 (2004) 393–98.

———. "Second Thoughts about Theologies of Hope." *Evangelical Quarterly* 72/4 (2000) 335–46.

———. *Song of Songs*. Interpretation: A Bible Commentary for Teaching and Preaching Louisville: Westminster John Knox, 2005.

———. "A Space for God." In *Mary, Mother of God*, edited by Carl E. Braaten and Robert W. Jenson, 49–57. Grand Rapids: Eerdmans, 2004.

———. *Story and Promise: A Brief Theology of the Gospel about Jesus*. Philadelphia: Fortress, 1973.

———. *Systematic Theology*. Vol. 1, *The Triune God*. New York: Oxford University Press, 1997.

———. *Systematic Theology*. Vol. 2, *The Works of God*. New York: Oxford University Press, 1999.

———. "A Theological Autobiography to Date." *Dialog* 46/1 (2007) 46–54.

———. *A Theology in Outline: Can These Bones Live?* Transcribed, edited, and introduced by Adam Eitel. Oxford: Oxford University Press, 2016.

———. *The Triune Identity: God according to the Gospel*. Philadelphia: Fortress, 1982.

———. "Theosis." *Dialog* 32/2 (1993) 108–12.

———. "Three Identities of One Action." *Scottish Journal of Theology* 6 (1975) 1–15.

———. "Toward a Christian Theology of Israel." *Pro Ecclesia* 9/1 (2000) 43–56.

———. *Visible Words: The Interpretation and Practice of Christian Sacraments*. Philadelphia: Fortress, 1978.

———. "What If It Were True?" *Neue Zeitschrift für Systematicsche Theologie und Religionsphilosophie* 43/1 (2001) 3–16.

———. "What Kind of God Can Make a Covenant?" In *Covenant and Hope: Christian and Jewish Reflections,* edited by Robert W. Jenson and Eugene B. Korn. Grand Rapids: Eerdmans, 2012.

Jenson, Robert W., and Solveig Lucia Gold. *Conversations with Poppi about God*. Grand Rapids: Brazos, 2007.

Knight, Douglas. "Time and Persons in the Economy of God." In *The Providence of God: Deus habet consilium*, edited by Francesca A.

Murphy and Philip G. Zeigler, 131–43. London: T. & T. Clark, 2009.

Lash, Nicholas. *Holiness, Speech, and Silence: Reflections on the Question of God*. Aldershot, UK: Ashgate, 2004.

Leithart, Peter. "Jenson as Theological Interpreter." In *The Promise of Robert Jenson's Theology: Constructive Engagements*, edited by Stephen Wright and Chris E. W. Green, 45–57. Minneapolis: Fortress, 2017.

Maximus the Confessor. *Two Hundred Chapters on Theology*. Edited by Luis Joshua Salés. St. Vladimir's Seminary Press Popular Patristics Series 53. Yonkers, NY: St. Vladimir's Seminary Press, 2015.

Moltmann, Jürgen. *The Coming of God: Christian Eschatology*. Translated by Margaret Kohl. Minneapolis: Fortress, 1996.

———. *The Crucified God: The Cross of Christ as the Foundation and Criticism of Christian Theology*. Minneapolis: Fortress Press, 1993.

———. "What Is Time? And How Do We Experience It?" *Dialog* 39/1 (2000) 27–34.

Nichol, A. W. *Exodus and Resurrection: The God of Israel in the Theology of Robert W. Jenson*. Emerging Scholars. Minneapolis: Fortress, 2016.

Pannenberg, Wolfhart. *Systematic Theology*. Vol. 3. Translated by Geoffrey W. Bromiley. Grand Rapids: Eerdmans, 1998.

Rahner, Karl. *Foundations of the Christian Faith*. Crossroad Paperback. New York: Crossroad, 1982.

Staniloae, Dumitru. *Eternity and Time*. Fairacres Publication 136. Oxford: SLG, 2001.

Steiner, George. *Real Presences: Is There Anything in What We Say?* New York: Open Road, 2013.

Tanner, Kathryn. *Jesus, Humanity, and the Trinity: A Brief Systematic Theology*. Minneapolis: Fortress, 2001.

Ware, Kallistos. *The Orthodox Way*. Rev. ed. Crestwood, NY: St. Vladimir's Seminary Press, 1995.

Wright, N. T. *Paul and the Faithfulness of God*. 2 vols. Christian Origins and the Question of God 4. Minneapolis: Fortress, 2013.

Wright, Stephen. *Dogmatic Aesthetics: A Theology of Beauty in Dialogue with Robert W. Jenson*. Emerging Scholars. Minneapolis: Fortress Press, 2014.

———. "The Creator Sings: A Wesleyan Rethinking of Transcendence with Robert Jenson." *Heythrop Journal* 53/6 (2011) 972–82.

Made in the USA
Middletown, DE
11 May 2021